SOCIAL INDICATORS

GARLAND REFERENCE LIBRARY
OF SOCIAL SCIENCE
(VOL. 62)

SOCIAL INDICATORS
An Annotated Bibliography of Current Literature

Kevin J. Gilmartin
Robert J. Rossi
Leonard S. Lutomski
Donald F. B. Reed

American Institutes for Research
Palo Alto, California

GARLAND PUBLISHING, INC. • NEW YORK & LONDON
1979

We are grateful for permission to reprint the following from
Psychological Abstracts:
   p. 14, from Vol. 52, 1974, No. 12388;
   p. 25, from Vol. 53, 1975, No. 02052;
   p. 30, from Vol. 40, 1975, No. 02073;
   p. 32, from Vol. 54, 1975, No. 11540;
   p. 41, from Vol. 57, 1977, No. 11379;
   p. 50, from Vol. 53, 1975, No. 08219;
   p. 54, from Vol. 53, 1975, No. 00086;
   p. 63, from Vol. 55, 1976, No. 02291;
   p. 68, from Vol. 57, 1977, No. 12441;
   p. 92, from Vol. 56, 1976, No. 07747;
   p. 104, from Vol. 49, 1973, No. 01390;
   p. 111, from Vol. 56, 1976, No. 03875;
   p. 113, from Vol. 56, 1976, No. 03884.
Copyright 1973, 1974, 1975, 1976, 1977 by the American Psychological Association. Reprinted by permission.

© 1979 by American Institutes for Research, Inc.
All rights reserved

Library of Congress Cataloging in Publication Data

Main entry under title:
   Social indicators.

   (Garland reference library of social science; v. 62)
   Includes indexes.
   1. Social indicators—Bibliography.   I. Gilmartin, Kevin J.
II. American Institutes for Research in the Behavioral Sciences.
Z7164.S66S52   [HN25]   016.309'07'2   78-67062
ISBN 0-8240-9755-6

Printed on acid-free, 250-year-life paper
Manufactured in the United States of America

CONTENTS

Preface   vii

Introduction   ix

Key Historical Works Published Prior to 1972   1

State-of-the-Art Overview of Social Indicators Research   10

Theoretical Approaches to Constructing Social Indicators   17

Methodological Approaches to Constructing Social Indicators   46

Analyzing and Reporting Social Indicators   79

Examples of Social Indicators Used or in Use   104

Bibliographies of Social Indicators Research   116

Author Index   119

Subject Index   123

PREFACE

The social indicators movement, some twelve years old, was motivated by the desire to create a system of social accounts—analogous to the existing system of national economic accounts—that would periodically assess levels of social wellbeing, determine the interactions among societal institutions, and measure the effects of governmental programs. Work in the social indicators area has progressed steadily along a variety of paths toward this goal. This progress has been chronicled in professional journals, social science information clearinghouses, and newsletters distributed to interested persons.

Six years ago, a major effort was made to organize summaries of research efforts in the social indicators area (Wilcox, Brooks, Beal, and Klonglan, 1972). Since that time, social indicators research efforts have continued and have increasingly aroused the interest of social scientists and policymakers. For example, the Social Science Research Council established its Center for Coordination of Research on Social Indicators in 1972, the international journal *Social Indicators Research* started publication in 1974, and the National Science Foundation established a separate research division on social indicators in 1977. Thus, it seemed that the time had come for another effort to compile an annotated bibliography of current (post-1972) literature on social indicators to supplement the earlier volume and to provide researchers and users in the area with an up-to-date reference guide.

The opportunity to compile an annotated bibliography of current social indicators literature was provided by the Youth Development Bureau, U.S. Department of Health, Education, and Welfare, under contract #105-77-2002. As an initial step in formulating a strategy for the Youth Development Bureau to use in constructing a series of social indicators to monitor the quality of youth development nationally, a bibliography of the social indicators literature was to be compiled. It was decided with the Government Project Officer, Dr. Darryl Summers, to expand this task and to produce a comprehensive, completely annotated bibliography of current work in the social indicators area. We are appreciative of Dr. Summers' support in organizing this volume.

Throughout the preparation of this annotated bibliography, the support of Nancy Carmichael, Librarian of the Social Science Research Council Center for Coordination of Research on Social Indicators, has been consistently helpful. We are also grateful to Ms. Emily Campbell for typing and overseeing production of this volume.

INTRODUCTION

This bibliography supplements the partially annotated compilation of references to works on social indicators prepared by Wilcox, Brooks, Beal, and Klonglan *(Social Indicators and Societal Monitoring: An Annotated Bibliography*, 1972).* The present collection does include a listing of key historical works on the subject published prior to 1972, with annotations provided for each work cited; however, we have chosen to focus on literature published during the period 1972-1978. This bibliography is the most comprehensive and the most extensively annotated one available on social indicators for this time period. While some of the abstracts were obtained from existing data bases and are so identified, every abstract that is included was reviewed and, where necessary, was revised or edited. Our aim in annotating all works cited and in taking such care to present the summaries of these works in as readable a form as possible has been to provide a resource material for persons working in the area of social indicators, whether they be statisticians, sociologists, economists, political scientists, psychologists, educational researchers, health researchers, or individuals operating from within a multifaceted frame of reference.

Compilation of the bibliography

Five approaches were followed in compiling this annotated bibliography. First, Lockheed's DIALOG system** was used to search six data bases: (1) National Technical Information Service

---

*Annotated reference is made to this bibliography in the "Bibliographies" section of the present monograph.

**DIALOG is a set of more than seventy data bases of machine-readable citations and abstracts of published materials. These data bases were searched interactively from a computer terminal at the American Institutes for Research.

Introduction • x

(NTIS); (2) Sociological Abstracts; (3) American Psychological Association, Psychological Abstracts; (4) Educational Resources Information Center (ERIC); (5) Social Science Citation Index; and (6) Comprehensive Dissertation Abstracts. Second, a working relationship was established with the Social Science Research Council Center for Coordination of Research on Social Indicators. With the help of the Center's library and experience in the field, many materials, some of which would otherwise likely have gone unnoticed, were identified and have been included. Third, all articles and books that were referenced in either the journal *Social Indicators Research* (published quarterly since 1974 by D. Reidel Publishing Company, Alex C. Michalos, editor) or the *Social Indicators Newsletter* (issued since 1973 by the Social Science Research Council Center for Coordination of Research on Social Indicators) were reviewed. Fourth, searches were made in several of the Stanford University libraries for materials indexed under titles such as "social indicators," "social accounting," "societal monitoring," and so on. Finally, our fifth approach was to locate the fugitive articles, books, reports, and other materials referenced in leading articles in the field. For example, materials were ordered from the Organization for Economic Cooperation and Development, the Association of Public Data Users, and the Economic Council of Canada, and contacts were made and orders for materials placed with the Gallup polling organization, the Foundation for Child Development, and the United Nations Economic and Social Council. Using these procedures, a listing of approximately 600 materials was identified. These materials were reviewed, and those only peripherally related to the topic of social indicators were deleted.

Organization of the bibliography

The bibliography is divided into seven major sections:
Key Historical Works Published Prior to 1972 (KH)
State-of-the-Art Overview of Social Indicators Research (SA)
Theoretical Approaches to Constructing Social Indicators (TA)

Methodological Approaches to Constructing Social Indicators (MA)
Analyzing and Reporting Social Indicators (AR)
Examples of Social Indicators Used or in Use (EX)
Bibliographies of Social Indicators Research (BB)

Within each section, references are listed in chronological order so that the reader may gain a sense of the development that has occurred to date in a specific area. Works published in the same year are listed alphabetically by author. Since references are numbered consecutively within each section, those references with higher numbers will be ones with more recent publication dates.

In the author index, the name of each author is followed by (1) one or more two-letter codes indicating the sections of the bibliography in which the person's works are located and (2) after each code listed, one or more numbers locating each work within the particular section. To find an author's most recent work in an area, the researcher has only to locate the citation with the highest number for that author in one of the sections. For example, if the author index included the listing

Doe, J. (SA) 2, 14, 26; (TA) 1, 5; (EX) 2

and one were interested only in Doe's most recent state-of-the-art review (SA), one would look up entry 26 in the "State-of-the-Art Overview of Social Indicators Research" section of the bibliography.

A subject index has also been provided; it follows the same conventions of codes and numbering as the author index. The subject index references citations by content areas in which social indicators may be developed and used (e.g., education, health). This indexing approach was selected to facilitate the development and the consideration of indicators for use in program- and policy-related activities (e.g., monitoring, evaluation).

The abstracts that are provided for each work cited were obtained from several sources. Sometimes the abstract was taken from one of the data bases accessed by means of DIALOG. In these cases, the abbreviated name of the data base follows the abstract (e.g., NTIS, PSYCH ABS, ERIC). When the abstract was written by one of the authors of this bibliographic listing, no reference is made to the source of the abstract.

Use of the bibliography

The author index, the subject index, and the seven section divisions may be used separately or together in searching for works on social indicators. In addition, the author index may be used to gain a better understanding of who are the individuals publishing most frequently in one or more areas of the field. The manner in which the sources of abstracts have been identified (e.g., NTIS, PSYCH ABS, ERIC) also allows the researcher to gain a better understanding of the type of information on social indicators contained in the major public and private clearinghouses. More generally, in providing references to the most recent and most important works on social indicators, the bibliography should enable researchers to utilize existing resources more fully in conceptually and operationally defining indicators and identifying methodologies for their development.

SOCIAL INDICATORS

KEY HISTORICAL WORKS PUBLISHED
PRIOR TO 1972

1. President's Research Committee on Social Trends. Recent social trends in the United States. New York: McGraw-Hill, 1933.

   This massive volume (1,568 pages plus xcv) is the report of President Hoover's Research Committee on Social Trends. An extensive preface reviews major policy problems facing the nation. Twenty-nine chapters follow, each presenting statistical trends in a different content area. The chapter on childhood and youth (50 pages), for example, covers the topics of vitality and health; medical care of children; the neglected and dependent child; the delinquent child; the child laborer; the schools; play, recreation, and religious education; parent education; and child research.

2. Moore, W. E., and Sheldon, E. B. Monitoring social change: A conceptual and programmatic statement. Social statistics proceedings of the American Statistical Association. Washington, D.C.: American Statistical Association, 1965.

   The authors discuss the monitoring of large-scale structural transformations in American society, the trends of these changes, and how public policy does and could affect those trends. Five major areas are suggested for monitoring: the demographic base, major structural components, distributive features, aggregative features, and welfare.

3. Bauer, R. A. (Ed.). Social indicators. Cambridge, Mass.: M.I.T. Press, 1966.

   In this second volume of the series prepared by the American Academy of Arts and Sciences for the National Aeronautics and Space Administration on the impact of the space program on American society, Raymond Bauer and his colleagues examine the need to anticipate the consequences of rapid technological change. Albert Biderman's chapter on social indicators and goals and Bertram Gross's chapter on social systems accounting are considered to be classics in the social indicators literature. Because of this book, Bauer has been referred to as "the father of the social indicators movement."

4. Biderman, A. D. Social indicators and goals. In R. A. Bauer (Ed.), Social indicators. Cambridge, Mass.: M.I.T. Press, 1966.

   The author discusses existing social indicators in terms of their relationships to national goals, the ways in which such statistical series originate, and the multiple uses to which they are put. One of Biderman's objectives is to convince the reader that the problem of inadequate and inaccurate statistics is indeed a serious one and not a matter of trivial technical niceties. Crime rates are taken as a case example of a set of indicators with such serious problems that we might be better off with no indicators at all than with the highly misleading ones that are used. Biderman explores the constraints on how we might set up an ideal set of social indicators for evaluating the state of society.

5. Gross, B. M. The state of the nation: Social systems accounting. In R. A. Bauer (Ed.), Social indicators. Cambridge, Mass.: M.I.T. Press, 1966.

In this chapter, a general model for an international system of national social accounts is presented. The model integrates relevant concepts developed by economists, political scientists, sociologists, anthropologists, psychologists, and social psychologists. According to the model, the state of any nation at any period of time can be analyzed in terms of two interrelated, multidimensional elements: system structure and system performance. This system of accounts is intended to be descriptive rather than explicitly explanatory, although it is hoped such a descriptive system will form the basis for explanation. A full system of national social accounting thus supplies the concepts needed to (1) structure information on the past or present; (2) formulate goals; and (3) establish criteria for evaluation. More generally, it is the author's view that such a system is a conceptual system through which people try to represent concrete systems. General structural elements identified include (1) differentiated subsystems, (2) internal relations, and (3) external relations. General performance elements identified include (1) acquisition of inputs, (2) production of outputs for external use, and (3) investments made in the system. Structural and performance elements of the model are broken down further into 20 and 21 more specific elements, respectively, and examples relevant to organizations and nations are presented. The author concludes by setting out some of the problems that will likely be encountered in developing social indicators, but stresses the usefulness of working from a comprehensive system description to development of indicators for particular subsystems.

6. Webb, E., Campbell, D. T., Schwartz, R. D., and Sechrest, L. Unobtrusive measures: Nonreactive research in the social sciences. Chicago: Rand McNally, 1966.

The authors review methods of obtaining social science research data by means other than interviews or questionnaires with the dual purpose of broadening social scientists' range of utilized methodologies and encouraging creative and opportunistic exploitation of unusual measurement possibilities. Their principal objection to the use of interviews and questionnaires is that they tend to be used alone and hence introduce systematic bias. These techniques should, therefore, be supplemented by methods that assess the same social science variables but introduce a different sort of methodological bias. In short, multiple operationalism is called for, and measurement strategies are introduced that (1) can cross-validate traditionally used procedures and (2) do not require the cooperation of a respondent and, therefore, do not themselves contaminate the response. General categories within which these measurement strategies are presented include (1) physical traces (i.e., erosion and accretion); (2) archival data

Key Historical Works (KH)

(both "running records" and episodic and private records); (3) simple observation; and (4) continued observation. Many examples of measures are presented.

7. Mondale, W. F. Some thoughts on "stumbling into the future." American Psychologist, 1967, 22, 970-973.

As author of the Full Opportunity and Social Accounting Act (U.S. Senate, 1967), Senator Mondale describes the lack of planning for tomorrow's results of today's change and how the Act would help alleviate some of those problems.

8. United States Senate. S.843: Full Opportunity and Social Accounting Act. American Psychologist, 1967, 22, 974-976.

This is the text of the Full Opportunity and Social Accounting Act as introduced on February 6, 1967, by Senator Walter F. Mondale and ten other senators. The Act would establish a President's Council of Social Advisors, require the President to submit an annual Social Report, and establish a Joint Congressional Committee on the Social Report.

9. United States Senate. Testimony before the Senate Subcommittee on Government Research of the Committee on Government Operations: Full Opportunity and Social Accounting Act. American Psychologist, 1967, 22, 977-1035.

Testimony concerning the Full Opportunity and Social Accounting Act is given by Gerhard Colm, National Planning Association; Herbert Gans, Center for Urban Education; Philip Hansen, University of Chicago; Robert Abelson, Yale University; Wilbert Moore and Eleanor Sheldon, Russell Sage Foundation; William Gorham, DHEW; Charles Zwick, Bureau of the Budget; Eli Rubinstein, NIMH; William Taylor, U.S. Commission on Civil Rights; Whitney Young, Jr., National Urban League; and Louis Harris, Louis Harris and Associates.

10. Cohen, W. J. Social indicators: Statistics for public policy. American Statistician, 1968, 22, 14-16.

The author, speaking as the Secretary of Health, Education, and Welfare, points out the need for two types of information that statisticians must supply to policymaking officials. These types are (1) statistics that help to identify and measure problems and (2) statistics that help decide how best to use available resources to solve these problems. "Social indicators" are referred to as statistics of the first type. The lack of indicators of the condition of society and the large number of statistics that simply record the activities of federal, state, and local agencies are particular areas of concern that are identified. Social indicators are also considered as a means for making issues understandable to the public. Once series of such indicators are developed, the author suggests that "social accounting" systems may be created and used to explain rises and falls in the indicators. In this way, social indicators will contribute to the availability of the second type of information noted above.

11. Sheldon, E. B., and Moore, W. E. (Eds.). Indicators of social change. New York: Russell Sage Foundation, 1968.

    This volume focuses on the theoretical and practical concerns of measuring large-scale structural change in the country. The chapters, by a variety of authors, discuss the major component parts of our society. The 13 content-specific chapters are categorized into four areas: (1) the demographic base, giving an indication of aggregative population trends and their changing composition and distribution across the nation's surface, (2) major structural components of the society, examining the ways in which our society produces goods, organizes its knowledge and technology, reproduces itself, and maintains order, (3) distributive features of the society, looking at how the products of the society are allocated across the American population, and (4) aggregative features of the society, the ways in which the system as a whole changes with respect to its inequalities, variable opportunities, and social welfare.

12. Bell, D. The idea of a social report. Public Interest, 1969, 15, 72-84.

    The author reviews the recent history and current state-of-the-art of social indicators and social reports, with particular emphasis on Toward a Social Report (USDHEW, 1969). The implications of various ways in which social reports could be produced in the future are discussed.

13. Duncan, O. D. Toward social reporting: Next steps (Russell Sage Foundation Social Science Frontiers Series, No. 2). New York: Russell Sage Foundation, 1969.

    The author expresses concern over the dangers that might occur if the initial and somewhat confused enthusiasm with social indicators is allowed to motivate promises of social accounting systems before such promises can be fulfilled. He thus is concerned with the steps that should be taken so that initial enthusiasm is not dampened and there is a "strengthening of commitment" among those who are called upon to do the work. Five "steps" are thought to be either the wrong ones to take or to have the lowest priority. These are (1) developing social accounts systems; (2) construction of composite indexes; (3) deciding what types of measures ought to be included in social reports; (4) deciding which agency should be responsible for publishing which social report; and (5) use of social indicators to evaluate social programs. The author considers the problem of measuring social change as the most immediate task to be performed. The positions of the "theorist" and the "inductivist" on this measurement issue are presented with the author opting for the latter approach on pragmatic grounds. He most strongly supports an approach to indicator development that combines the use of existing data with those that are newly collected. This approach is termed "replication of base-line studies," and it is pointed out that this approach (1) should have the greatest marginal return for a given input of resources and (2) should be encouraged since it is the strategy least likely to be adopted in the ordinary course of events. Examples of replication studies and guidelines for conducting such studies are presented.

14. Educational Policy Research Center. Toward master social indicators (SRI project 6747, Research Memorandum EPRC-6747-2). Menlo Park, Calif.: Stanford Research Institute, 1969.

Key considerations in the development of a comprehensive national social data system are described. Processes for aggregating low-level indicators into composite indicators ("master indicators") are proposed. The authors present tables of attainment categories, subcategories, and possible indicators for each of seven areas related to the individual and society.

15. Ferriss, A. L. Indicators of trends in American education. New York: Russell Sage Foundation, 1969.

Statistical time series on various aspects of education are presented along with discussion of the interpretation of the trends, criteria for the selection of an indicator, and different types of statistical series. Topics include enrollment, teachers, quality of education, graduates, trends in educational organization and finance, and educational attainment.

16. Gross, B. M., (Ed.). Social intelligence for America's future: Explorations in societal problems. Boston: Allyn and Bacon, 1969.

The chapters in this book are the reorganized and slightly revised articles previously published in two volumes of The Annals of the American Academy of Political and Social Science (371 and 373, May and September, 1967) with Bertram Gross as Special Editor. In these chapters, a varied group of scholars, government officials, and journalists explore what is--or what they think should be--going on in a wide variety of specialized fields. One of the purposes of this collection, apart from probing the particular content areas, is to illuminate the variety of approaches to social indicators and goals. The 20 chapters were written by ten sociologists, five political scientists, three journalists, three economists, one law professor, and one physician.

17. Olson, M. Social indicators and social accounts. Socio-Economic Planning Science, 1969, 2, 335-346.

This paper defines "social indicators" as statistics that have two defining characteristics. They are, first, measures of direct normative interest; that is, what the economist would call measures of "welfare" and "illfare." The second defining characteristic of a social indicator is that it should fit into a systematic scheme of classification or aggregation that would make possible a balanced assessment of socioeconomic progress or retrogression in some broad area, as well as disaggregated and detailed study of particular problems. The work in government on social indicators was designed in part to meet the needs of Toward a Social Report, a preliminary study of the condition of American society issued by the U.S. Department of Health, Education, and Welfare (1969). Social indicators can also fit, with other statistics, into a set of "policy accounts" or scheme of social accounting, which would relate social expenditures to the social indicator they were designed to affect. This would encourage broadened cost-benefit analysis and rational public decisionmaking. The author concludes that, although a complete set of policy accounts is a utopian goal at present, work on developing policy accounts should not be postponed. Only a systematic, theoretical approach that starts with the informational requirements of public policy will do; the author believes that social indicators and policy accounts as he has defined them provide such an approach.

18. United States Department of Health, Education, and Welfare. Toward a social report. Washington, D.C.: U.S. Government Printing Office, 1969.

The title of this volume was chosen to indicate that it is not a social report, but rather a step in the direction of a social report and the development of a comprehensive set of social indicators. What is known about progress toward generally accepted goals is presented for several areas: health, social mobility, the physical environment, income and poverty, public order and safety, and learning, science, and art. There is also a chapter on participation in social institutions, but because of the lack of relevant indicators in this area, it aspires to do no more than pose important questions.

19. Box, G. E. P., and Jenkins, G. M. Time-series analysis: Forecasting and control. San Francisco: Holden Day, 1970.

The book is concerned with the building of models for discrete time-series and dynamic systems. It describes in detail how such models may be used to obtain optimal forecasts and optimal control action. All the techniques are illustrated with examples using economic and industrial data. In Part I, models for stationary and nonstationary time-series are introduced, and their use in forecasting is discussed and exemplified. Part II is devoted to model building and procedures for model identification, estimation, and checking, which are then applied to the forecasting of seasonal time-series. Part III is concerned with the building of transfer function models relating the input and output of a dynamic system computed by noise. In Part IV, it is shown how transfer function and time-series models may be used to design optimal feedback and feedforward control schemes. Part V contains an outline of computer programs useful in making the needed calculations and also includes charts and tables of value in identifying the models.

Key Historical Works (KH)

20. Central Statistical Office. Social trends (Nos. 1-4). A publication of the Government Statistical Service, M. Nissel (Ed.). London: Her Majesty's Stationery Office, 1970, 1971, 1972, 1973.

For four consecutive years, statistical charts and time-series were published, describing the status in a number of public policy areas for England and Wales, Great Britain (including Scotland), and the United Kingdom (including Northern Ireland). The content areas are population, employment, leisure, personal income and wealth, personal expenditure, health and personal social services, education, housing, environment, justice and law, and resources. The final section in each publication compares the United Kingdom to other countries on a number of indicators.

21. Ferriss, A. L. Indicators of change in the American family. New York: Russell Sage Foundation, 1970.

Statistical time-series on various aspects of the American family are presented. Topics include marriage rate, marital status, households, fertility, dependency, divorce, work and income, and poverty.

22. Land, K. C. Social indicators. In R. B. Smith (Ed.), Social science methods. New York: Free Press, 1970.

This state-of-the-art paper presents the theoretical and methodological issues in the development and use of social indicators. The distinctions between social indicators, social reporting, and social accounting are explained. The author explores the potential uses of social indicators for public policy, and describes a macro measurement approach similar in methodology to macro-economic models.

23. Sheldon, E. B., and Freeman, H. E. Notes on social indicators: Promises and potential. Policy Sciences, 1970, 1, 97-111.

The authors claim that the concept of social indicators continues to be diffuse and that there are exaggerated claims of the utility of indicators. Deficiencies in both conceptualization and method limit the potential of indicators for such tasks as priority setting and program evaluation. Moreover, the development of social accounts, based on the analogy with economic accounts, is fallacious. Redirection in effort and more realistic claims can reduce the possibility of an eventual decline in work on indicators and enhance the value of the movement for both policymakers and social scientists concerned with the analysis and prediction of social change.

24. Terleckyj, N. E. Measuring progress towards social goals: Some possibilities at national and local levels. Management Science, 1970, 16, B765-B778.

In order to fill gaps in policy-relevant information needed by decisionmakers, the author points out that existing information can be organized and provided on a more regular basis to meet many of these needs and, for other needs, serious work can be initiated to develop information, improve existing information, and communicate information more effectively. Twenty indicators are selected, including life-expectancy at birth and the number of persons with chronic disabilities as the indicators reflecting health goals, the rate of violent crimes as the measure of public safety, and the number of persons in poverty or near-poverty as indicative of concerns with equity. The author notes that most of the information had to be pieced together, since existing statistical systems are not geared to provide it. Gaps in information were found in several areas, including quality of the physical environment and use of discretionary or leisure time. Although locally collected data can be meaningful, augmenting existing nationally collected data, the author concludes that more complete reporting systems and systems aimed at assessment of possibilities for future changes require much additional basic and developmental work.

25. Ferriss, A. L. Indicators of trends in the status of American women. New York: Russell Sage Foundation, 1971.

Statistical time-series on various aspects of the lives of women are presented. Topics include education, marital status, fertility, labor force status, income, health, and recreation. The author does not find relations between these statistics and the rise of protest movements and related feminist endeavors, and he explores other plausible hypotheses.

26. Forrester, J. W. Counterintuitive behavior of social systems. Technological Forecasting and Social Change, 1971, 3, 1-22.

The author argues that our social systems are far more complex than our technological systems and that we do not know enough to design the most effective social systems directly without first going through a model-building experimental phase. It is often the case that actions we assume will alleviate a social problem actually would exacerbate it in the long run. A computer model of world system dynamics is presented and explored, with simulations from the present to the year 2100 of the changes in quality of life, population, pollution, and a number of other variables as a function of policies affecting levels of capital investment, use of natural resources, and other variables.

27. Land, K. C. On the definition of social indicators. American Sociologist, 1971, 6, 322-325.

The author reviews the claims that have been made for social indicators and the criticisms of those claims. Various definitions of social indicators are reviewed and criticized, and the author offers an alternative definition involving the indicator serving as a parameter or variable in a social systems model. Two classes of social systems models are discussed, those that deal with the aggregate levels or amounts of various social activities and those that attempt to determine the distribution of the activities among the various elements of the society.

Key Historical Works (KH)

28. Rivlin, A. M. Systematic thinking for social action. Washington, D.C.: Brookings Institution, 1971.

The author reviews the current ability to answer four questions that would and should be of concern to decisionmakers. These questions relate to (1) definition of problems, (2) definition of persons to be served by social programs, (3) definition of programs that are effective in meeting needs, and (4) strategies for increasing program effectiveness. She points out that considerable progress has been made in providing answers to Questions 1 and 2, while little or no progress has been made with regard to Questions 3 and 4. A major conclusion is that analysts who want to help improve social service delivery should give high priority to developing and refining measures of performance. She suggests that development of these measures should (1) avoid reliance on single performance measures and (2) reflect the difficulty of the problem.

29. Sheldon, E. B. Social reporting for the 1970s. Volume II, Federal statistics: A report of the President's Commission. Washington, D.C.: U.S. Government Printing Office, 1971.

The state-of-the-art of social indicator development is reviewed, and three types of social indicators are distinguished: (1) problem-oriented indicators, which are intended for direct use in policy and program decisions, (2) descriptive indicators, intended primarily to describe the state of society and the changes taking place within it, and (3) analytic indicators, which serve as components of explicit conceptual and causal models of social systems. Criteria for social indicators and the linkage of social indicators to social policy are discussed. Current practices and proposed developments are described for two illustrative content areas: (1) public safety and legal justice and (2) youth. Recommendations are made for the future development of social indicators.

STATE-OF-THE-ART
OVERVIEW OF SOCIAL INDICATORS RESEARCH

1. Brossman, M. W. Quality of life indicators: A review of state-of-the-art and guidelines derived to assist in developing environmental indicators. Washington, D.C.: Washington Environmental Research Center, 1972. (NTIS No. PB-225 034/8)

    The report provides a review and assessment of the state-of-the-art of quality of life indicators. Economic indicators, social indicators, environmental indicators, and an all-encompassing quality of life indicator are discussed. The report traces the history of each category of indicator development, discusses the difficulties found, and suggests guidelines for future indicator development. (NTIS)

2. Bubeck, A. E. International perspectives on social welfare research: A report of an international symposium. Washington, D.C.: Brookings Institution, 1972. (NTIS No. PB-216 596/7)

    Proceedings of the 1971 international symposium on social welfare research show a concern for the lack of international data in the field of social welfare and a need for exchange of such information. Papers and discussions at the symposium included reports from individual countries and discussion of such topics as the need for social indicators, building of a data base, the role of social welfare in policy-making, and the role of international bodies such as the United Nations. The symposium concluded with a series of proposals for furthering the international exchange of social welfare information and experiences. (NTIS)

3. Oborn, P. T. Review of the literature on social indicators. Denver: Denver University Social Welfare Research Institute, 1972. (NTIS No. PB-238 853/6ST)

    The report contains a review of the literature on social indicators up to 1972. There is heavy emphasis on factors related to social indicator methodology (i.e., subjectivity, evaluatory criteria, validity, and reliability). A brief reformulation of the reviewed material appears in the final section, and a summary consideration of the author's perspective appears at the end of each major section and in the conclusion. Footnotes and bibliographies are also included. (NTIS)

4. Parke, R., and Sheldon, E. B. The need for social indicators. Proceedings of the 25th Annual Meeting of the Industrial Relations Research Association, 1972, 99-105.

    The authors review the state-of-the-art of social indicator development. Topics include exploitation of existing data resources, demographic and social accounts, models of social systems, and subjective indicators of the quality of life.

State-of-the-Art Overviews (SA)

5. Plessas, D. J., and Fein, R. An evaluation of social indicators. Journal of the American Institute of Planners, 1972, 38(1), 43-51.

This review article examines some of the current diverging views on social indicators as well as some of the major problems facing social indicator development. The article calls for more data, more practical suggestions, and more rigorous theoretical formulations.

6. Sheldon, E. B., and Land, K. C. Social reporting for the 1970s: A review and programmatic statement. Policy Sciences, 1972, 3(2), 137-151.

The article reviews the state-of-the-art of social indicators research. The authors state that the interest in social measures of this type is due largely to the demand for information relevant to (1) policymaking, (2) monitoring the well-being of society, and (3) modeling aspects of the social system. The distinction between objective and subjective measures of the quality of life is discussed, and the fact that the definition and measurement of well-being requires a comparative perspective is noted. Elements that play a key role in linking social measurements to social policies are delineated, as are three criteria for the selection of areas to be measured or of particular measures themselves. The authors review the work that has been accomplished in developing social indicators in the areas of public safety, legal justice, and youth. They then present several recommendations that would extend work in these and other areas of social concern. Among these recommendations are (1) a research and development strategy; (2) an organizational structure for the conduct of social indicators research; and (3) coordinating mechanisms that will monitor and coordinate activities, both within and outside of government.

7. Zapf, W. Social indicators: Prospects for social accounting systems. Social Science Information, 1972, 11, 243-277.

The author presents a chronology of major events in the social indicators field in the United States and concludes that initiatives for comprehensive social reporting have tended to come from the following groups: parliamentarians pressing for data collection in connection with legislation; governmental agencies or committees that make surveys and propose priorities, especially in crisis situations; research institutes engaged in independent social reporting; and international organizations seeking to implement standardized information systems. Developments in the field of empirical societal analysis are reviewed, including cross-national and longitudinal comparisons of nations, futurology (long-term forecasting), cost-benefit analysis and the Planning-Programming-Budgeting System (PPBS), and societal simulation. The author describes the political orientation of the social indicators movement and characterizes it as "liberal incrementalism." Nine available social reports are reviewed and summarized in an extended table, and some instructive differences regarding theoretical conception, content, and presentation are disclosed. The author expresses disappointment that the crucial subjects of economic and political power structures, interest representation and lobbying, elite

11

recruitment, economic concentration and monopolization, armaments, ghetto riots, and social conflicts in general are almost completely omitted from social reports. Various alternatives and controversies concerning the construction of social indicators are presented and discussed. The author suggests indicators that should be developed in the major content areas and supplies relevant references for the indicators that are not straightforward. The prospects for social accounting systems are discussed, and obstacles to adequate data use are described: nonscientific uses of statistics, cultural lag in statistics, and built-in inflatory bias. Three designs for integrated systems of social accounts are presented (Gross, 1966; Stanford Research Institute, 1969; and Stone, 1970), and a structure-performance model of society is discussed. The author concludes that the efforts to start social reporting and social accounting have proved to be not quite as difficult as had been supposed.

8. Dunn, E. S. The national data bank movement in the United States. Proceedings of the Business and Economic Statistics Section of the American Statistical Association. Washington, D.C.: American Statistical Association, 1973.

This article is a critical review of the national data bank movement in the United States. It considers the Ruggles Committee Report, the Dunn Report, and the Kaysen Committee Report. The author points out that, at present, this movement is not making progress. He argues that both the data bank movement and the currently popular social indicators movement have not, in their interest in statistical reform, considered the issues of statistical system design. According to the author, proponents of both these movements believe that information problems can be solved by reapplying extant procedures to a wider range of needs and problems with more efficiency. He argues that this belief is questionable and that statistical reform must be conceived of in a broader fashion.

9. Moss, M. (Ed.). The measurement of economic and social performance. New York: National Bureau of Economic Research, 1973.

This volume is a collection of the papers and comments presented at the Conference on the Measurement of Economic and Social Performance held at Princeton in 1971. The papers reflect a variety of concerns, but focus on the problem of providing a more accurate measure of performance than that offered by the current system of economic accounts. Particular attention is given to the following two questions: (1) Should the measurement of economic performance extend beyond the enterprise economy so as to include (a) the production of households, (b) an evaluation of environmental resources and conditions, and (c) the services supplied by government? and (2) Should the measurement of the economic performance of enterprises itself be modified in significant ways? One section of the volume is devoted to the topic of measuring the amenities and disamenities of economic growth.

State-of-the-Art Overviews (SA)

10. Duncan, O. D. Developing social indicators. Proceedings of the National Academy of Sciences, 1974, 71(12), 5096-5102.

    Recent progress in developing social indicators is described in terms of six activities. In regard to social bookkeeping, the number of domains covered by population surveys is being expanded, and survey data are being more widely disseminated. In social accounting, demographic stock-flow schemes show promise of integrating systems of social statistics. Social science theories have provided models of achievement and other social processes. Social forecasting is potentially an important component of work on social indicators, but a new definition of the purpose of forecasting is needed. The practice of social reporting is best exemplified in the work of recent commissions. Social advising, while it draws upon social indicators, involves functions that cannot be performed by any system of indicators alone. The author concludes that the long-run effect of developing social indicators is not calculable; however, social indicators have the power to alter our fundamental ideas about human desires and possibilities, which in turn may change society.

11. Goeke, J. R. Some neglected social indicators. Social Indicators Research, 1974, 1, 85-105.

    The attention now being given in the social sciences to time series data that measure the "social health" of the nation is considered a most welcome development. Too often, sweeping claims of social change have very little hard supporting evidence. Thus, the author feels that the new trend indicators offer the opportunity for more rigorous analysis of diverse subjects than other measures that are customarily employed in the "soft sciences." Indicator trends are reviewed in the following areas: (1) politics, (2) business, (3) ecology, (4) labor, (5) job satisfaction, (6) youth, (7) religion, and (8) population size and growth. The indicators were not selected systematically, but were ones the author felt had been overlooked by social indicators researchers and sociologists generally and by policymakers. Public opinion indicators show a decline in favor for United States business, which has resulted in congressional legislation on business, labor reform, restrictions on the environment, consumerism, and inflation. More restrictions can be expected if the social indicators are correct. Political indicators tell us that Republican party loyalty and allegiance have steadily declined since the 1950s and perhaps the "emerging Republican majority" is merely a myth. There are vast implications to be derived from indicators that show the birth rate nearing zero population growth and religion steadily losing influence in America over the past 30 years. The author also believes that indicators would show that youth are far more sober than the rebellious few who draw mass media attention. Social indicators have been very predictive of the future, but many important indicators have been largely ignored. It is suggested that a clearinghouse is needed to systematically monitor existing social indicators in order to avoid waste, duplication, and downright neglect of important information.

12. Gross, B. M., and Straussman, J. D. The social indicators movement. Social Policy, 1974, 5(3), 43-54.

   The authors examine different foci, cross-currents, and future orientations of the social indicators movement that are the result of heterogeneous interests and needs. Foci are shown to range from the simple collection or analysis of social information to the articulation of social goals, the preparation of social reports, and the development of social accounts. The cross-currents include noneconomist professionalism, broadband economism, humanism, statisticism, conceptualism, radicalism, and managerialism. The future orientations point toward a more tightly managed corporate society, on the one hand, and a more humanist, democratic, egalitarian postindustrialism, on the other. Examination of these elements of the indicators movement is made from both historical and political perspectives.

13. Hamburger, P. L. Social indicators: A marketing perspective. Chicago: American Marketing Association, 1974.

   This monograph includes a review and analysis of social indicators that are used to assess the quality of life as it pertains to marketing theory and strategy. Topics include the historical development of social indicators, theories of consumer behavior, assumptions of the capitalistic economic system, human wants, marketing performance, general equilibrium and welfare assumptions, and criticisms of marketing and consumerism. (PSYCH ABS)

14. Van Dusen, R. A. International social indicators: An overview of ongoing activities. St. Louis, Missouri: International Studies Association Meeting, 1974. (ERIC No. ED 091 263)

   International social indicators, focusing on assessment of quality of life, measurement of social changes, and program evaluation, are the subject of this paper. Beginning with a look at various national reports that are currently being produced, it is felt that these documents and the data gathering activities upon which they are based form the bulk of much of what is known about international social indicators. The same national reports, furthermore, confront many of the methodological and substantive issues that must be faced in cross-national projects with social data. The major activities involved in using international social indicators are comparison of conditions in various countries, cross-national programs of data collection, and multinational programs of data collection. The major portion of the paper presents an outline of some major international projects and a discussion of some ongoing data collection activities that will provide important new information to the field of international social indicators. Discussion focuses on potentially comparative studies, using juxtaposition of national data and cross-national data collection. Tables illustrate social changes in Japan and a typology of international social indicators. (ERIC)

15. Land, K. C. Theories, models, and indicators of social change. International Social Science Journal, 1975, 27, 7-37.

   The author reviews the history of the social indicators movement from its inception in the 1960s in the United States and describes the major contributions to the field. Five definitions of social indicators and problems with those definitions are presented, and the author reviews his own alternative definition and conceptual framework. Land's general framework for development of social indicators, which classifies indicators as being policy instrument descriptive indicators, nonmanipulable descriptive indicators, social system analytic indicators, output end-product descriptive indicators, second-order impact analytic indicators, or side-effect descriptive indicators, is used to illustrate the shortcomings of traditional social system model-building procedures. The author discusses how social indicators can be validated externally either by a social policy criterion or by a social change criterion, and he differentiates between two types of macro-sociological time series social indicator models, those concerned with the aggregate level of well-being and those concerned with equity. An alternative kind of model based on individual-level data (sociological life-cycle social indicator models) is described.

16. Parke, R., and Carmichael, N. Recent research on social indicators. The New York Statistician, 1975, 27(1), 3-4.

   This article is a brief overview of work in the social indicators area. It recommends that researchers in this area (1) pursue empirical research, (2) make use of extant data, (3) employ advanced analytic techniques, (4) use probability sample surveys, (5) use replicated cross-section surveys, (6) employ techniques like cohort analysis which illuminate repeated cross-sectional data sets, (7) focus on national trends, and (8) not limit their conception of social change to those factors subject to manipulation by public policy.

17. Quantifying the unquantifiable. MOSAIC, 1975, 6(5), 2-9.

   This article describes recent research attempting to develop a body of social indicators that would gauge the quality of life. Most of this research is conducted by federal agencies and relates to indicators that measure the well-being of individuals and families rather than of governments or institutions. (ERIC)

18. Sheldon, E. B., and Parke, R. Social indicators: Social science researchers are developing concepts and measures of change in society. Science, 1975, 188, 693-699.

   This article reviews significant milestones and products associated with the "social indicators movement." Four areas of activity are highlighted: (1) statistical time series to measure social change, (2) evaluation research and social experimentation, (3) net national welfare measurement, and (4) national goals accounting. While the authors review recent attempts at improving the data bases in these areas, they warn that attempts to use social indicators in social accounting, social engineering, or evaluation efforts may be misguided. They conclude that the development and analysis of descriptive time series and the modeling of social processes are the most promising approaches to describing the state of society.

19. Zapf, W. Systems of social indicators: Current approaches and problems. International Social Science Journal, 1975, 27, 479-498.

Ten examples of operational social indicator systems from various countries are described. For each system, the following seven aspects are specified: (1) research objective, (2) system, (3) method of selection and weighting, (4) goal areas or life domains, (5) type and number of indicators, (6) data base from which the indicators were constructed, and (7) topics. With the aid of the examples, some general problems are discussed: (1) the functions of social reporting (measurement, evaluation, accounting, explanation, and innovation), (2) the nature of social indicators, and (3) the levels of analysis and components of welfare that enter into the analysis of welfare. The author concludes with a description of the SPES Project financed by the German Research Association and being carried out by the Social Policy Research Group of Frankfurt/Mannheim.

20. Obudho, R. A. Social indicators for housing and urban development in Africa: Towards a new development model. Social Indicators Research, 1976, 3, 431-449.

The main goal of this article is to stimulate discussion among African scholars and government officials about social indicators as means of measuring economic, political, and social progress (as opposed to using GNP-type measures). A review is made of the literature on social indicators, and it is demonstrated that this literature can be applied to measuring the (social) progress in urban and housing development in international, national, regional, and local environments. The author believes that social indicators can be successfully used to evaluate the degree of progress that is being made in achieving a wide range of social goals in Africa.

21. Zapf, W. International, public, and private actors in social reporting. Washington, D.C.: Social Science Research Council Center for Coordination of Research on Social Indicators, 1976.

The author reviews the efforts of three nations to develop and institutionalize social reporting. The influences of international organizations as well as public and private actors on these efforts are described. The danger that social reporting could become a one-way flow of controlled information is noted, and the desirability of a two-way exchange between the public and private sectors is stressed. Such a two-way exchange is possible only if social scientists outside the government have guaranteed access to public data resources.

22. Miller, R. B. Social indicators: Tools for evaluation, or for the study of social change? New York: Annual Meeting of the American Educational Research Association, 1977. (ERIC No. ED 138 626)

The evolution of the social indicators movement is described, focusing particularly upon the split between those who hold that indicators are statistical time series for the measurement of social change and those who look to social indicators for evaluations of government programs. In addition to discussing these two positions and their impact on the social indicators movement, the paper points out the implications of each position for the development of indicators in the field of education. (ERIC)

THEORETICAL APPROACHES
TO CONSTRUCTING SOCIAL INDICATORS

1. Allardt, E. A frame of reference for selecting social indicators. Commentationes Scientiarum Socialium, 1972, 1, 1-16.

    This paper is an attempt to relate some of the objectives of social indicators to sociological distinctions and theory. The points of departure are (1) that nations are input-output systems and (2) that output must be assessed in terms of individual needs. Five "elements of society" are defined--one input component, two structural, and two output components. A set of four "goal dimensions" are elaborated from Maslow's hierarchical classification of needs. These two sets of categories are then cross-classified to create a matrix of 20 theoretical variables or indicator types. Since this model depends heavily on the notion of a "need," clarification is offered by a functional analysis of need as a homeostatic variable subject to modifications by control variables and tension variables. Further, a distinction is made between want-regarding and ideal-regarding principles for public policy. It is pointed out that needs, as homeostatic variables, are societally defined. It follows that one area for research is the social definition of the tolerance limits of such homeostatic variables and that no set of indicators can be established once and for all.

2. Campbell, A., and Converse, P. E. (Eds.) The human meaning of social change. New York: Russell Sage Foundation, 1972.

    This book was commissioned by the Russell Sage Foundation as a companion piece to Indicators of Social Change (Moore & Sheldon, 1968). Whereas Moore and Sheldon were concerned with various kinds of hard data, typically sociostructural, this book is devoted chiefly to so-called softer data of a more social-psycholocial sort: attitudes, expectations, aspirations, and values. The purpose was to set forth a statement of the most significant dimensions of psychological change, a review of the state of information regarding them, and a projection of the measurements needed to improve understanding of these changes in the future. Topics include community, family and kinship, work, leisure, the American electorate, and Negro population, the criminal justice systems, and alienation.

3. Environmental Protection Agency, Office of Research and Monitoring. An anthology of selected readings for the Symposium on the "Quality of Life" Concept: A potential new tool for decision-makers. Washington, D.C.: Author, 1972. (ERIC No. ED 069 600)

    The selected readings in this anthology deal with the quality of life (QOL) concept in general as well as from the more specific perspectives of environment, economy, society, and psychology. The articles represent varying approaches and levels of consideration and were selected to serve as a general briefing for participants in the Quality of Life Symposium sponsored by the EPA. The objective of the symposium was to explore the QOL concept, to define QOL in terms of its components, and to develop suggested quantitative approaches to its use in guiding public policy. The articles are classified under the following five topics: (1) defining quality of life measures--the state of the art; (2) the quality of life concept; (3) QOL: environmental perspectives; (4) QOL: economic and social perspectives; (5) QOL: psychological perspectives. Since this anthology was prepared as a general briefing rather than a review of the literature, a list of suggested readings is included at the end of the work. (ERIC)

4. Freeman, H. E. Outcome measures and social action experiments: An immodest proposal for redirecting research efforts. The American Sociologist, 1972, 7(9), 17-19.

The author suggests that neither normative social indicators nor psychological properties should be used as dependent variables in social action experiments and evaluations. Sociologically normative measures are overly biased by our culture, and psychological measures are similarly subject to cultural bias and tend to be even further removed from observation than measures in sociology. The author proposes that interest in outcome measures be redirected to a different set of dimensions, in particular measures of an individual's social viability. Social viability, the competence of individuals to achieve their ends through the social system, is a universal measure without the usual cultural biases. Social action programs should be evaluated in terms of their ability to increase the social viability of individuals.

5. Girardeau, C. Social indicators. Social Science Information, 1972, 11, 229-242.

The author distinguishes between social indicators and socioeconomic accounts and discusses the areas of overlap between the two. The purpose of social indicators, like socioeconomic accounts, is to interpret and express the complexity of social reality through a limited number of relations and to summarize an increasing volume of statistical information. The author states that past disappointments with social indicators have shown that the construction of indicators should be the end-product of a long effort of analysis and research in a particular area; it is this prior research and theorizing that distinguishes between social indicators and social and demographic statistics. Areas of analysis for social indicators can be (1) society as a whole, analyzed in terms of its social heterogeneity and its evolution; (2) collective services (e.g., health, education); or (3) horizontal areas not clearly linked to a collective function (e.g., social mobility, solidarity, adaptation to change, special population groups). The author concludes by discussing reasons why social indicators cannot be developed in certain content areas.

6. Girardeau, C. Toward a system of social statistics. Social Science Information, 1972, 11, 189-202.

The author describes the evolution of demand for social information, including both demands expressed by public authorities and latent demand. Four major methods of studying social phenomena are identified and described: (1) the organization of statistics around themes, (2) the creation of satellite accounts, (3) the construction of

Theoretical Approaches (TA)

sociodemographic systems, and (4) the development of social indicators. The author states that none of these approaches can provide the essential framework for a complete system of social statistics by itself, but together they meet a large part of the demand. A diagram is presented that indicates how these four approaches are mutually supporting, and the author suggests that the four approaches should be developed simultaneously in such a way that research on one approach will be beneficial to the development of the other approaches.

7. Henriot, P. J. Political aspects of social indicators: Implications for research. New York: Russell Sage Foundation, 1972. (ERIC No. ED 103 460)

The author proposes that social indicators are basically a matter of values, of interest, of policies--hence of politics. Thus, complementing the current focus on the structural and social-psychological aspects of measuring social change, we find here a statement and research approach relating social measurement to antecedent and consequent political considerations. It is also stated that all measures of the quality of life have implications for public policy and thereby may well have political impact. The author suggests that the frontiers of research be expanded so as to develop new "political indicators," to examine systematically the needs for and use of indicators, and to investigate the institutional arrangements for their production. The approach of this report is a mixture of discussion and research agenda. While assuming some previous acquaintance with the literature, a background and explanation to highlight specific political aspects of the topic are provided. In the first half of the study, a framework for political research into the social indicators movement is considered; in the second half, an agenda of suggestions for particular areas of research by social scientists is outlined. (ERIC)

8. Hjerppe, R., and Niitamo, O. E. Social indicators as an information and cognition system of social conflicts. Instant Research on Peace and Violence, 1972, 1, 34-41.

When developing a conceptual framework within which to construct social indicators, one can either (1) examine the welfare of individuals in various need categories or (2) examine the resources available for individuals. To measure welfare or level of living is a very complicated matter; either one can assume that every individual knows what is "good" and "best" for himself/herself and this can be found out by making an inquiry, or one can try to explain "scientifically" the hierarchy of human needs. The authors conclude that a more meaningful approach is to study the distribution of available resources among individuals. The problem of operationalizing the basic goals of social policy is discussed. The authors point out three major dangers in the construction of a system of social indicators: (1) the danger of quantification--all the essential information cannot be quantified, and what is quantifiable is not necessarily an unbiased sample of the essentials; (2) the danger of values--the values underlying the operationalization may not be explicit or even recognized; and (3) the danger of inelasticity--the conceptual framework for the system of social indicators may not be elastic enough to incorporate new features and to eliminate old ones on the basis of improved understanding of the social system.

9. Hughes, J. W. Urban indicators, metropolitan evolution, and public policy. New Brunswick, New Jersey: Rutgers University Center for Urban Policy Research, 1972.

   This work is a study of metropolitan areas in the United States that aims to provide a set of indicators reflective of urban conditions. A conceptual framework is presented that is based on general systems theory and the concept of metropolitan evolution. Metropolitan evolution, it is hypothesized, begins with traditional, dispersed settlements and ends with dispersed, total urbanization and high levels of consumption. Methods of urban analysis that are considered include the Shevky-Bell dimensions, Park's theory of urban ecology, Hoyt's sector model, and factor analysis. The study uses the Standard Metropolitan Statistical Area as its basic observational unit.

10. Spautz, M. E. The socioeconomic gap. Social Science Research, 1972, 1, 211-229.

    A timely and relevant prototype model is presented to illustrate how social indicators might be statistically combined into an overall "Index of Social Health" for the United States. (ERIC)

11. Allardt, E. A welfare model for selecting indicators of national development. Policy Sciences, 1973, 4(1), 63-74.

    This paper presents a frame of reference for selecting social indicators on the basis of values inherent in the concept of social welfare. The author suggests that these values constitute three categories: Having, Loving, and Being. There is a rough correspondence between this tripartite classification of values and Abraham Maslow's need-hierarchy (1943). Having corresponds to Maslow's first two need categories (physical needs and safety needs), loving entails his third and fourth categories (love needs and esteem needs), and being relates to his fifth category (self-realization needs). A scheme for selecting indicators is presented by crosstabulating the basic value categories with elements of society. National societies are conceived of as systems in which there are inputs, outputs, and a structure through which inputs and feedbacks flow. The inputs and outputs on the different value-dimensions can be assessed through measures of central tendencies, whereas structure can be described through dispersion parameters and correlations. Dispersion indicates the extent of equality in a society, and correlations indicate the extent of justice.

12. Arnold, W. R. A social report for central portions of the Kansas City area. Kansas City, Missouri: Mid-America Urban Observatory, 1973. (NTIS No. PB-234 753/2)

    The report is designed to serve policymakers and citizens concerned about the guidance and assistance that local governments may give to service systems. The report (1) provides a rationale for conceiving of three kinds of hindering processes that detract from the quality of life for the populace and (2) presents facts about services that can keep these processes from hindering individuals' full participation in the society. Each of the three processes is conceived to be reciprocal between the citizens whose quality of life is restricted and the organizations designed to maintain or restore the capacity of these citizens as full participants in their community. (NTIS)

13. Barker, R. G., and Schoggen, P. *Qualities of community life: Methods of measuring environment and behavior applied to an American and an English town.* San Francisco, California: Jossey-Bass, 1973.

This volume is the result of an effort to develop an ecological psychology of human action. It describes in detail the changes over a decade in the living conditions of an American and an English town and the behavior that these conditions engender. Of particular interest are the concepts and methods employed by this study for assessing quality of life. These include measures of habitat variety and stability, use of habitat extent as a measure of resources, the notions of a site genotype and of the erosion and expansion of such genotypes, and characterization of genotypes in terms of attendance attributes, inhabitant attributes, action pattern qualities, and degrees of autonomy.

14. Economic Planning Centre. *Quality of life: Social goals and measurement.* (Summary of a study of social indicators made by a Division of the Economic Council of Finland) Helsinki: Author, 1973.

The work of six groups within the Economics Planning Centre is described. Each group was assigned a particular area of well-being for which social indicators or a system for generating social indicators was to be defined. The six areas were (1) health, (2) education, (3) physical environment, (4) inequality, (5) housing, and (6) working conditions. The specific approaches followed and their results differed considerably, although the aims of the groups were the same. In particular, there was agreement that social indicators (1) should describe the state of a problem area and the factors believed to affect this state, (2) should form a bridge between goals for each area and its state-description, and (3) should identify the importance of statistical information already available.

15. Finsterbusch, K. The sociology of nation-states: Dimensions, indicators, and theory. In M. Armer and A. D. Grimshaw (Eds.), *Comparative social research: Methodological problems and strategies.* New York: John Wiley & Sons, 1973.

This paper is an effort to bring into focus the study of nation-states. Comparative macrosociology tends to examine either primitive societies, in total or by institutions, or the major institutions of nation-states such as the military, the polity, the economy, the educational system, and science. The study of nation-states as wholes, still a near-monopoly of the historians, is relatively undeveloped as a sociological discipline. This paper suggests two dozen variables for the sociology of nations, discusses their measurement, constructs a causal theory that postulates their interrelationships, considers the validity of the theory, and finally reduces that theory to more manageable proportions.

16. Gitter, A. G., and Mostofsky, D. I. The social indicator: An index of the quality of life. Social Biology, 1973, 20, 289-297.

The authors review several issues that figure importantly in the development of social indicators. How is the concept "quality of life" to be understood? What sorts of objective and subjective indicators are needed to assess this concept, and how are they to be interrelated? How should one determine those quality of life components that are the most important? The authors present a social indicator measurement model that is based on the life encounters of a single person over time. The model would assess the individual's satisfaction with respect to 16 dimensions of quality of life (e.g., health, educational attainment), using both objective and subjective measures for one or more time periods. An example is presented of how one would use the model in constructing one or more social indicators for a quality of life dimension. The authors note that, while only output indicators can be used to assess quality of life, input indicators are an integral part of social accounting systems. A summary checklist of questions is presented that the authors feel social indicators researchers should address in their work.

17. Johnstone, J. N. Indicators of the performance of educational systems (IIEP Occasional Paper No. 41). Paris: International Institute for Educational Planning, 1973.

In this paper, discussion is restricted to indicators of educational system performance. By "educational system" is meant that system that is formally established within a country for the purpose of providing education according to the UNESCO definition of the term. What is said generally applies to indicators in other fields of the social sciences as well as to social and development indicators in general. The paper begins by establishing a theoretical model within which educational indicators can be defined and by discussing certain conceptual problems concerning the purposes for which indicators might be used and the methodological problems encountered in forming indicators. After a review of educational indicators developed to date, the paper develops a core of ten educational indicators and demonstrates two approaches to using them to map educational systems performance across and within nations. The paper concludes by outlining research that may be conducted to extend both the core of indicators and the methodology proposed. (ERIC)

18. Organization for Economic Cooperation and Development. Indicators of performance of educational systems. Washington, D.C.: OECD Publications Center, 1973. (ERIC No. ED 087 677)

This report is an outline of a system of indicators for evaluating the performance of educational systems and grows out of OECD work

Theoretical Approaches (TA)

on social indicators. Existing statistical data on education consists of "inputs." The desire expressed in this study, however, is to measure "outputs," or actual system performance. Whenever a relationship exists between a statistical measure of education and a notion of welfare or well-being, it is called, for the purposes of this report, an indicator (i.e., it measures output or performance). After a short introductory chapter, the second chapter discusses approaches and methods toward the selection of goals and the evaluation and construction of indicators. Possible goal areas in education discussed in Chapters 3-7 are transmission of knowledge and skill, education and the economy, equality of educational opportunity, provisional educational services for individual requirements, and education and the quality of life. These chapters make precise statements about the different emphases that are possible inside a general area and, within those subareas, discuss possible indicators and the assumptions required for their construction. When a specific indicator emerges from the consideration of goals, the policy implications of its variation are discussed. (ERIC)

19. Organization for Economic Cooperation and Development, Directorate for Manpower and Social Affairs. <u>List of social concerns common to most OECD countries: The OECD social indicator development programme.</u> Washington, D.C.: OECD Publications Center, 1973. (ERIC No. ED 081 702)

This document is a report of the Manpower and Social Affairs Committee of the OECD on the development of a set of social objectives with the general goals of (1) identifying the social demands, aspirations, and problems that are or will likely be major concerns of socioeconomic planning processes; (2) measuring and reporting change relative to these concerns; and (3) focusing and enlightening public discussion and governmental decisionmaking. In this report, the Working Party on Social Indicators identifies, selects, and specifies a list of 24 fundamental social concerns common to most member countries. Concepts and principles for the selection of common social concerns are defined, and the significance and applicability of the selected concerns are discussed. The concerns listed are developed according to the following basic criteria: (1) concerns that are of present or potential interest to member governments; (2) fundamental human aspirations or concerns as opposed to means or instrumental aspects of well-being; (3) major, essential aspects of well-being. Notes which clarify the meaning of words and concepts used in the list of social concerns are included. (ERIC)

20. Sismondo, S. <u>Social indicators for policy research and democratic action: A paradigm and some examples.</u> (Report 73-119.) New York: Joint Meeting of the American Sociological Association and the Rural Sociological Society, 1973. (ERIC No. ED 082 908)

The primary purpose of this paper is to present a possible means to establish a new social indicators intelligence system that embodies a relations testing capacity. Major ideas defined and described include social indicators, theory, model, policy research, and democratic action. A paradigm covers the movement from theory to model and action. Three examples are used to show the inference from model to reality. It was noted that a system for the construction, collection, and analysis of social indicators should not be isolated from other intellectual and political endeavors. It is argued that a single best utilization of social indicators research exists within the policy research and analysis domain that will respect the functioning of the democratic system. (ERIC)

21. United Nations Department of Economic and Social Affairs. Social indicators for housing and urban development: Report of the ad hoc group of experts. New York: United Nations, 1973. (United Nations Document ST/ECA/173)

This report presents a frame of reference for developing and interpreting social indicators of housing. The report (1) considers the content and components of housing indicators, (2) discusses direct and indirect indicators, (3) points out the importance of nonstructural characteristics, (4) suggests some promising indicators, and (5) discusses the kinds of data most urgently needed to improve measurement of standards for the "housing environment." The report concludes with a list of the working papers presented by the ad hoc committee.

22. United States Environmental Protection Agency. The quality of life concept: A potential new tool for decision-makers. Washington, D.C.: Author, 1973.

This volume is the report of a symposium sponsored by the Environmental Protection Agency. The symposium's objectives were (1) to define the quality of life concept in terms of its components and (2) to suggest quantitative approaches to the use of the concept in guiding policy decisions. Section I of the volume summarizes the results of the symposium and elaborates the issues reviewed in its course. Section II is an anthology of 17 papers that were presented at the symposium.

23. Biderman, A. D., and Drury, T. F. Self-perceived social value and moral qualities of one's work: Neglected social dimensions for quality of employment indicators. Washington, D.C.: Bureau of Social Science Research, 1974. (NTIS No. PB-256 874 9ST)

Measures are proposed of the impacts workers see their work having on others and the degree to which they feel their work has or lacks various moral qualities. Such measures would have significance not only from the conventional economic, individualistic, hedonistic, and behavioral perspectives underlying most quality-of-work indicators, but also to the extent that these social and moral considerations enter importantly into workers' overall evaluations of their jobs. From a societal viewpoint, measures of self-perceived social and moral job qualities and of the importance workers attach to them constitute important social indicators in their own right. (NTIS)

24. Bradburn, N. M. Is the quality of working life improving? How can you tell? And who wants to know? Studies in Personnel Psychology, 1974, 6(1), 19-33.

This paper examines the concepts behind the variables involved in the changes in the quality of working life and the role of the United States government in monitoring these changes. The focus is (1) on the relation of aspects of working life to a general theoretical framework for how people come to judge themselves as happy or unhappy and (2) on the role of social indicators in government policy formulation. (PSYCH ABS)

25. Christian, D. E. International social indicators: The OECD experience. Social Indicators Research, 1974, 1(2), 169-186.

One effort to develop an operational set of international social indicators was sponsored by the Organization for Economic Cooperation and Development. This article describes the OECD plan and makes a preliminary appraisal of the completed first phase of the work. During this phase, the definition of the elements of well-being for which specific indicators of change should be developed were identified. Attention is directed to certain aspects of the overall strategy being pursued by OECD, including its delimitation of scope to the one type of social indicators (termed "well-being indicators") on which international agreement appears to have been achieved. A possible governmental strategy for the development of a more comprehensive system of social indicators is suggested.

26. Clemhout, S. Assessment of consumer research for a valuation of a quality-of-life policy. Social Indicators Research, 1974, 1, 329-357.

This article evaluates the allocation, coordination, priority assignments, and new directions of research efforts aimed at a consumer policy. Since the author argues that the consumer welfare should be central to the political-economic system, a detailed analysis of the primary elements of this system that interrelate to produce possible levels of welfare are examined. In-depth consideration is devoted to five points: (1) consumer choice and freedom, (2) controls available to consumers over their environment, (3) the demographic characteristics of consumer populations over the life-cycle, (4) the interaction between the individual and the group emerging from the hierarchies of influence at the individual, group, and societal levels, and (5) structure of the markets, degree of concentration, and business practices related to sales. As a result of this analysis, the author presents three recommendations for a strategy for consumer policy. First, clear priorities should be determined in allocating resources to meet consumer problems. Second, integrative measures should be devised to deal with the multifaceted policy measures needed to manage, if not eradicate, certain problems facing the consumer. Third, quality-of-life components should be recognized and given special attention. It is suggested that interdisciplinary efforts could foster a consumer policy that would be part of a more encompassing quality-of-life policy.

27. Dubin, R. Indicators of the responsiveness of employment systems to workers' needs and values. Irvine, Calif.: University of California, 1974. (NTIS No. PB-256 871/5ST)

    This paper sets forth some general criteria that social indicators of the quality of working life need to meet, indicates some specific criteria involving workers' needs and values, and makes some suggestions for the development of several possible social indicators. There are at least four important considerations involved in the development and use of social indicators: that the purposes of social indicators be kept in mind, that the reality being measured be acknowledged and understood, that values be specified that represent good and bad on the indicator, and that the possibility be taken into account that the social indicators employed will be an instrument for a self-fulfilling prophecy. The criteria for judging workers' needs and values can be grouped into three classes: personal safety and creature comfort, social and psychological well-being, and the worker-citizen nexus. The development of social indicators of the quality of working life from the standpoint of workers' needs and values is examined with respect to five separate topics: values surrounding work, opportunities for individual mobility, welfare redefinition, psychological freedom, and the worker as a consumer. (NTIS)

28. Elinson, J. Toward sociomedical health indicators. Social Indicators Research, 1974, 1, 59-71.

    The author argues that the various forms of mortality data and biomedical measures of morbidity have become inadequate measures of the level of health in economically developed countries. Reports of functional physical disability have some advantages, but do not necessarily reflect physical disablement. Sociomedical health indicators reflect current attempts to move beyond these more traditional health status measures. They imply an assessment of a valetudinarian individual's condition in relation to others. The author states that an important way of looking at the purposes of these measures is to indicate the extent to which medical knowledge is being applied in a given society or to a specified population. Current attempts to develop sociomedical health indicators include measures of social disability; typologies of symptoms, which can be used to estimate probable needs for care; measures that focus on behavioral expressions of sickness; research based on operational definitions of "positive mental health," "happiness," and perceived quality of life; and assessments of met and unmet needs for health care, which are measures of social capacity to care for the sick. Sociomedical indicators reflect both objective conditions and social values. They are policy-oriented, serving as mobilizing agents for sociopolitical pressures concerned with raising the overall level of health of the population.

29. Fox, K. A. Social indicators and social theory. New York: John Wiley and Sons, 1974.

    The author proposes a system of social accounts and indicators, drawing on concepts from sociology, economics, and ecological psychology. Theoretical models are proposed that combine economic and noneconomic variables and are applied at the national and community levels and to higher education and earnings as a function of occupation. The author discusses some illustrative models of a world economy and the manner in which economic policies adopted by one nation affect prices and incomes in other nations. The history of the development of econometrics is summarized and compared to the situation in social indicators and models.

30. Henderson, D. W. Social indicators: A rationale and research framework. (Economic Council of Canada Monograph, Catalog No. EC22-2274) Ottawa: Information Canada, 1974.

This study focuses on the approach to social indicator development being employed by the Social Indicators Group of the Economic Council of Canada. Basic goal areas, derived from Maslow's categories of needs, are broken down further into subsystems. Next, the outputs for various subsystems are defined and a detailed taxonomy of outputs for each subsystem is described. The third step is essentially analytical, involving the determination of factors that may affect these outputs and their relative weights. Final steps include determination of programs and policies that affect key inputs, entering output measures from various subsystems into a production function related to a higher-level goal, and defining principal social indicators for each goal area. The author suggests that future critical areas of concern that will need to be monitored can be derived by "filtering" goal areas (or subsystems) through a matrix of four basic social trends. A list of concerns is presented, and weights are defined and associated with each area.

31. InterStudy. Indicators of the status of the elderly in the United States. Minneapolis: Author, 1974. (NTIS No. HRP0013845/3ST)

The status of the quality of life for elderly persons in the United States is assessed in a report that is also concerned with a conceptual methodology for defining and interpreting social indicators. The report is directed to executives charged with improving the quality of decisions in the Administration on Aging, DHEW; to professionals interested in social indicator methodology; and to persons interested in the status and problems of the elderly. The status report is presented in sets of social indicators for economic status, health status, social involvement, cultural norms and values influencing the quality of life, and cohort characteristics of the elderly population (as of the early 1970s). The conceptual and methodological approach used to determine the sets of social indicators and the relevant data is discussed both generally and in regard to each of the indicator categories. Generally, the approach taken is to define social indicators according to their relevance to the problem-solving capabilities of the elderly. Special attention is given to the extension of this approach to support federal policy decisions in the area of housing for the elderly. Specific methods used to refine definitions of indicators are (1) the use of role as an approach to the meaning and measurement of social interaction, (2) the identification of socially instituted or reinforced barriers to satisfactory patterns of living, and (3) the analysis of intrinsic problem-solving capacities developed by the elderly. Supporting data and a bibliography are provided. (NTIS)

32. Knox, P. L. Social indicators and the concept of level of living. The Sociological Review, 1974, 22, 249-257.

In contrast to what he terms the "recent and rather vague notion of the quality of life," the author proposes the concept of "level of living." He points out that level of living has a long doctrinal history and is relatively well defined by statistical reports produced in various countries. Noting that the meaning of the concept depends upon the context in which it is used, the author reviews several contexts that have been used and proposes a definition of level of living for Britain. He feels that a commonly accepted conceptual basis, such as the one proposed, must exist in order that operational or functional social indicators can be developed. Two guidelines are offered for defining level of living in other contexts: (1) it would be unsound to attempt to construct indicators of level of living that were based only on monetary criteria, and (2) level of living itself can therefore only be assessed in relative, rather than absolute, terms. Brief attention is paid to index construction, and the author suggests that a single level of living index should be disaggregatable into its constituent components and that the weights of individual components should be determined by the society whose level of living is being measured.

33. Krieger, M. H. Social indicators and the life cycle. Ekistics, 1974, 37, 277-283.

In this article, the life cycle is treated as a context within which indicators are developed at a general level. Stages of individual development, derived from Erikson, are presented, but indicators depend only on the structure and theoretical interdependence of these stages. Formulas are presented for three indicators: (1) whole life indicator, (2) mortality indicator, and (3) indicator of the cost to the society of unsuccessful development. Application of the "life cycle approach" to program evaluation is illustrated by an hypothetical example based on what social programs ought to do to facilitate individual development. Available data, drawn from several sources, are used to suggest real-world applicability. The author argues that the use of life cycle indicators would effectively allow a broad range of social programs or other interventions to be considered at one and the same time in relation to particular development stages.

34. Laszlo, C. A., Levine, M. D., and Milsum, J. H. A general systems framework for social systems. Behavioral Science, 1974, 19(2), 79-92.

In this paper, the relationship between general systems theory and social systems is explored, including an introduction to the general system characteristics that are basic to all systems. The basic dynamic properties of systems are described in terms of time lags or inertia, time delays, positive feedback or growth, negative feedback or homeostasis, stability, and thresholds. Building on these basic concepts, the authors describe control systems, optimization and performance criteria, and complex and hierarchical systems. Emphasis is placed on the discussion of social indicators and social accounts in the social theoretic context.

35. Morss, E. R. The revolutionary and the marginal-positivist: Does the social indicators movement open up a new possibility for dialogue? Social Indicators Research, 1974, 1(2), 229-242.

The author argues that a deep schism exists within the social sciences between the "marginal-positivist," who feels meaningful change can be made through marginal steps in our social systems, and the "revolutionary," who feels fundamental alterations are needed before our systems will work for the betterment of mankind. This essay asks whether social indicators are compatible with the methodologies of each group, and if so, whether they offer a new possibility for a fruitful dialogue. The author notes that the revolutionary would benefit from engaging in the social indicator movement, since he or she would be forced to specify his/her goals concretely, measure progress toward these goals, and consider alternative approaches to achieving the goals. The marginal-positivist, on the other hand, would benefit from such engagement in that working with social indicators would cause him or her to adopt a broader focus on societal problems. Since, in the author's opinion, persons holding either the revolutionary or marginal-positivist perspectives will benefit from involvement in the social indicators movement, he concludes that social indicators offer hope for constructive dialogue between persons holding these two perspectives.

36. Quinn, R. P. Strategy issues in the development of quality of employment indicators. Ann Arbor, Michigan: University of Michigan Survey Research Center, 1974. (NTIS No. PB-256 873/1ST)

This paper discusses several general strategy issues that must be confronted in the development of social indicators systems in general and systems for monitoring quality of employment in particular. The concept of quality of employment is defined, and two types of data collection are distinguished. Four types of measures are also distinguished, with the one most used being employers' reports of dollars spent on fringe benefits. The "quality-effectiveness" strategy was evolved in response to deficiencies in other measures. It defines three concepts: working conditions, effectiveness, and quality of employment. The "fit" model and the "standards" model of working conditions are examined in terms of the contradiction between the analytical and the descriptive goals of a monitoring system. (NTIS)

37. Seashore, S. E. Job satisfaction as an indicator of the quality of employment. Social Indicators Research, 1974, 1(2), 135-168.

In this article, it is suggested that the quality of employment should be assessed from the value perspectives of the employer and of society as well as the perspective of the worker. The prevailing conception of the nature of job satisfaction, and the associated measurement methods, provide useful but unnecessarily limited indicators of the quality of employment. An enlarged conception is offered as to the nature of job satisfaction, its causes, and its possible consequences. The implications of this conception for the utility of satisfaction measures as social indicators are examined as to three aspects: (1) the psychology of job satisfaction, (2) the sociology of job satisfaction, and (3) the approach and technology of using subjective satisfaction measures in conjunction with other indicators. The view is expressed that direct measures of subjective job satisfaction are an essential component in any effort to make comparisons or monitor changes in the quality of employment, but that such measures, like other subjective and objective indicators, have ambiguous meaning if used alone. Specific uses for social indicators of job satisfaction in increasing understanding of the work system are suggested. These include (1) determining the set of personal values (preferences) that are used by workers in evaluating their present employment, their motivation to change, and their choice of actions, (2) tracing the delayed and diffused work-related consequences of substandard conditions of employment, and (3) tracing the impact of substandard conditions of employment on other aspects of the lives of workers (e.g., family life). The relevance of social indicators for program planning and assessment is also reviewed.

38. Stolte-Heiskanen, V. Social indicators for analysis of family needs related to the life cycle. Journal of Marriage and the Family, 1974, 36, 592-600.

This paper describes a conceptual framework for the analysis of relationships between the family and the larger social system. The framework makes use of the concepts of social policy or social indicators as "linking mechanisms" between the family and the social system. The history of the social indicators movement is briefly outlined, and the author distinguishes between the "matter-oriented" and the "idea-oriented" uses of these measures. These two approaches are considered as reflecting the dual sense of social indicators: (1) they make possible the modification of society through the dissemination of concise information (matter-oriented), and (2) they are tools for expanding our scientific understanding of reality (idea-oriented). This paper takes an idea-oriented perspective and conceives of social indicators as empirical measures of inputs into societal subsystems (e.g., the family) that either reflect feedback responses to the changing needs of the family or aim at modifying the structure, function, goals, and so on of the subsystem. The two fundamental input-output linkages between the family and the society that are considered are those concerned with (1) the reproduction of the potential labor force and (2) the "ideological apparatus of the society." The analysis of these mechanisms, which reflect societal inputs in response to subsystem needs, is proposed as a method for combining analyses of macrolevel and microlevel phenomena.

39. Walton, R. E. QWL indicators: Prospects and problems. Studies in Personnel Psychology, 1974, 6(1), 7-18.

The article suggests that employees in North America are becoming less satisfied with the quality of their working lives (QWL). This quality of working life can be analyzed on three levels:

organizational conditions, employee attitudes, and behavioral systems. Additional social dynamics complicate the role of social indicators. A step model is presented for improving the quality of working life. (PSYCH ABS)

40. American Philosophical Society. Ecology of child development: Proceedings of the American Philosophical Society, 1975, 119(6), in toto. (ERIC No. ED 129 967)

This collection includes five papers dealing with different foci on the ecology of child development. The first presentation discusses childhood social indicators as means of monitoring the ecology of development. The second, on the social context of childhood, shows that how society treats its youngest members depends both upon its perception of what children are like and its perception of what is required for effective functioning of society itself. The value of children to parents and the decrease in family size is the subject of the third paper. This paper notes that in order to predict fertility trends, and birth rates, one needs to understand the motivational factors underlying the desire to have children and to analyze these motivations in relation to other social conditions--such as analyzing the needs that children satisfy, as well as costs (both emotional and financial) that are involved in parenthood. The fourth paper, on "reality and research in the ecology of human development," documents the changes over time that have been taking place in one enduring context that is critical for human development--the family. The final paper focuses on mounting effective child advocacy. (ERIC)

41. Baumheier, E. C., Oborn, P. T., Conner, L. I., Slaughter, E. L., and Cook, C. L. Toward a comprehensive data bank for social indicators. Denver: Denver University, Center for Social Research and Development, 1975 (NTIS No. SHR-0000523).

A conceptual framework defining a set of social indicators is presented that could be used to measure status as well as change in several areas of social concern. A composite list of social concerns drawn from the social indicators literature is discussed, and operational definitions are developed and compared to data presented in the Social Indicators Project of the University of Denver's Center for Social Research and Development in order to identify content gaps and to fix the limits of social indicators collection. The proposed comprehensive indicator system is designed to monitor change in quality of life with respect to economic, political, social, cultural, and environmental components. The data system is designed to handle information collected at the county level, but it could be disaggregated to the community or aggregated to the state level without presenting serious problems. It is pointed out that, although a comprehensive indicator system at the county level would present some practical difficulties in data collection, the system would provide benefits to county-level planners as well as to state and federal decisionmakers because it calls attention to change in all the domains of human experience. An appendix describes the Social Indicators Project and contains a bibliography. (NTIS)

42. Brand, J. The politics of social indicators. British Journal of Sociology, 1975, 26(1), 78-90.

   The author discusses the development of social indicators in terms of their relation to policy goals and their use by political organizations. In constructing indicators, the link between them and policy goals is often unclear because policy goals are not explicit. In addition, goals change over time, and indicators may not be relevant to the changed policies. Social indicators may be used by political organizations to vindicate their policies or as political weapons against opponents. (PSYCH ABS)

43. Brim, O. G., Jr. Macro-structural influences on child development and the need for childhood social indicators. American Journal of Orthopsychiatrics, 1975, 45, 416-524.

   The term "childhood social indicators" refers to statistical time series data that measure significant characteristics of child development. The author notes that such indicators require that there be identical measures, repetitively applied over time to comparable populations of children. In particular, these indicators should be focused on "macro-structural" influences on child development: economics, cultural values, politics, law, and sociology. "Micro-" and "meso-" structural influences are also described. Survey methodology is advanced as the method of developing childhood social indicators, and the importance of an interdisciplinary approach to the design and conduct of surveys is noted. While concerns for protecting the privacy and "humanness" of children participating in such surveys are expressed, the author points out safeguards that can be used. Current and prospective efforts to develop childhood indicators using survey techniques are reviewed.

44. Bunge, M. What is a quality of life indicator? Social Indicators Research, 1975, 2(1), 65-79.

   Elements of the environment affecting the quality of life for an individual are discussed. The concept of such indicators is examined, with an indicator being defined as a token or symptom of a particular condition. A social indicator is considered to be a variable for use in sociological studies. The social indicator concept is formalized mathematically, and sociological variables are also quantified in mathematical terms. Quality of life indicators are categorized as being physical, biosocial, psychological, technical, economic, social, political, and cultural. It is concluded that elements affecting the quality of life pertain to the individual/environment interface. The environment is the aggregate of both physical and social environments of an individual. The recommendation is made that further study be conducted to determine what statistics are relevant to the quality of life, since knowledge of the quality of life will not be increased merely by obtaining additional social and environmental statistics. (NTIS)

Theoretical Approaches (TA)

45. Edwards, J. Social indicators, urban deprivation, and positive discrimination. Journal of Social Policy, 1975, 4(3), 275-287.

   The author states that the use of social indicators in the implementation and monitoring of positive discrimination programs (in particular, programs to combat urban deprivation) is increasing and is likely to continue to do so, and therefore it is important that some of the unintended consequences of their use be appreciated. First, urban deprivation has never been adequately defined: it is at best an ambiguous term, and its nature and manifestations are constantly shifting. The application of precise and statistical techniques to such an ambiguous area is about as meaningful as "using a micrometer to measure a marshmallow." Second, urban deprivation is a miserable human condition, and politicans, administrators, and social scientists have no moral qualifications that enable them to measure fine degrees of misery. The author argues that there are two serious consequences of the usual empirical approach to the development and use of social indicators. First, it has diverted attention away from the need to define clearly what is meant by deprivation. Second, by assuming a consensus of opinion as to what constitutes deprivation, it has delayed recognition of the fact that social indicators and the social programs of which they may be a part are neither objective nor value-free. The author concludes that, by concentrating on technical and statistical problems, a gloss of objectivity and value freedom has been laid on an issue that is both conflictive and potentially politically divisive.

46. Flanagan, J. C., and Russ-Eft, D. F. An empirical study to aid in formulating educational goals. Palo Alto, California: American Institutes for Research, 1975.

   This study focuses on the effects of educational experience on an individual's quality of life in relation to the importance placed on particular dimensions of quality of life. The study used the "critical incident technique" with a national sample of persons to derive 15 dimensions of quality of life. To assess current status on quality of life, a nationally representative sample of men and women were chosen from the Project TALENT survey (ensuring the availability of background data). Participants were interviewed to gather information on their experiences, decisions, and perceptions related to the various dimensions of quality of life, and their current satisfaction vis-a-vis each dimension was determined. The study pinpoints the following areas of educational practice that should be developed further: (1) vocational guidance, (2) quality of teaching, (3) individualized instruction, (4) curriculum, and (5) personal support and guidance.

47. Fontane, P. E. Improving program evaluation with reciprocal indicators. Social Indicators Research, 1975, 2, 211-221.

   Recent interest in social indicators of change has emphasized the unidimensional monitoring of social programs. In this article, reciprocal indicators are presented and it is argued that these indicators permit the recording of two-dimensional, or contrasting, trends within a selected system, thereby providing efficient evaluation of program effectiveness. A religious indicator of congregation size is used to illustrate the differences between these two forms of indicators. The unidimensional indicator of congregation size is given by the differences over years in the sums of the annual gross church membership and the number of names added to the congregation during the years minus the number of members who have left the congregation during this period. The reciprocal indicator of congregation size that is presented is the percent total membership changed per year. Use of this reciprocal measure demonstrates that while, for the example considered, there was overall size stability, a substantial change in the membership population was taking place. The author suggests that reciprocal indicators may be useful for monitoring the effectiveness of affirmative action programs to attract qualified employees from minority groups (e.g., the number of minority group members actually hired divided by the number of qualified minority applications received) and for monitoring workers' use of leisure time (e.g., the number of workers on R&R activities divided by the number of workers earning additional income). Reluctance of social program designers to adopt reciprocal indicators is anticipated since such indicators (1) present program effectiveness in terms of a "mixed bag" and (2) may be used incorrectly to forecast program effectiveness.

48. Land, K. C. The role of quality of employment indicators in general social reporting systems. American Behavioral Scientist, 1975, 18, 304-332.

The author reviews the history of the social indicators movement from its inception in the 1960s in the United States and describes the major contributions to the field. Five definitions of social indicators and problems with those definitions are presented, and the author reviews his own alternative definition and conceptual framework. Land's general framework for development of social indicators, which classifies indicators as being policy instrument descriptive indicators, nonmanipulable descriptive indicators, social system analytic indicators, output end-product descriptive indicators, second-order impact analytic indicators, or side-effect descriptive indicators, is used to suggest how quality of employment indicators might be developed.

49. Levy, S., and Guttman, L. On the multivariate structure of well-being. Social Indicators Research, 1975, 2, 361-388.

In this article, a formal definition for the universe of well-being items that were part of the spring and summer trimesters of 1973 of the Continuing Survey in Israel is proposed. Results of empirical, multivariate research guided by this formal definition are presented. In effect, a partial theory for the structure of intercorrelations among the varieties of well-being is presented. The term "theory" refers in this case to an hypothesis of a correspondence between a definitional system for a universe of observations and an aspect of the empirical structure of those observations, together with a rationale for such an hypothesis. Supplementary data from an earlier trimester and data from the United States serve as partial replications for confirmation of the theory. A mapping sentence is used to express the study design. This sentence specifies and interrelates the universe of items and the population studied. According to this sentence, the assessment of well-being can be composed entirely of attitudinal items. Correlation matrices for well-being items for a population at a single point in time are analyzed by smallest space analysis (SSA). This analysis reveals that the structure of the interrelationships among the variables is that of intermeshing cylindrexes in an SSA space of four dimensions. Areas of life (e.g., recreation, education) play the role of polarizing facets, while self-versus-community and situation-versus-treatment serve as axial facets. Modulating facets include primary-to-secondary interaction and generality-to-specificity interaction. Happiness was found to be closest to variables that relate to the respondent's internal and social primary environment. The feeling of well-being in physical aspects cannot predict personal happiness as well as can sociopsychological aspects of life. Well-being items also were found to correlate more with the stratum of self than with the stratum of community.

50. Markley, O. W., and Bagley, M. D. Minimum standards for quality of life. Menlo Park, California: Stanford Research Institute, 1975. (NTIS No. PB-244 808/2ST)

The study addresses a number of issues of concern under various sectors of man's environment. For each issue three types of available information are compiled: (1) public laws and other less formal understandings that set minimum standards, (2) objective data that reflect how well those standards are being met, and (3) subjective data that reflect how people feel about that aspect of the quality of their life. Man's needs are grouped into two major areas: (1) basic needs, including minimal life conditions necessary to meet physiological and security needs, and (2) higher needs, to include social needs, ego needs, and a need for self-fulfillment. Standards are categorized under each major need area, according to three levels of concern, arranged in a hierarchical order: first, the existing welfare concern--a statement of the threshold level; second, security--standards ensuring the welfare for all persons; and finally, ability to influence--standards that allow individuals to influence threshold levels and their own access to welfare. (NTIS)

51. McCall, S. Quality of life. Social Indicators Research, 1975, 2, 229-248.

This article offers a definition of quality of life (QOL). While QOL has been defined by others in terms of actual happiness or perceived satisfaction/dissatisfaction, the present paper defines it as the presence of the necessary conditions for happiness throughout a society. Since idiosyncratic conditions for happiness are identified as a determinant of the sufficiency of any set of conditions for a happy state, those conditions that are identified for the general population are necessary but not sufficient conditions. High QOL is thus compatible with actual unhappiness. These conditions for happiness are necessary for the satisfaction of human needs rather than human desires. A Maslowian analysis of the former is proposed in default of any more satisfactory analysis. The paper concludes with a discussion of how maximizing need-satisfaction (as opposed to want-satisfaction) automatically guarantees fair distribution of needed goods This ensures that, to a degree, high-QOL societies are societies characterized by justice.

52. Rao, M. V. Socio-economic indicators for development planning. International Social Science Journal, 1975, 27, 121-149.

The author, who is joint director of the Central Statistical Organization of the Government of India, uses his country as a case study for construction of social indicators used in development planning. The development and use of social indicators in formulating the Indian Draft Fifth Five-Year Plan is described under the following topics: (1) health, family welfare, and nutrition, (2) urban development, housing, and water supply, (3) education, (4) employment, manpower, and labor welfare, (5) development of backward classes, (6) cooperation and community development, and (7) backward and special areas including hill and tribal areas. The author discusses problems with current indicators in these areas, presents a set of principles that should govern the selection of indicators, and proposes a set of indicators (based on these principles) suitable for purposes of development planning. These indicators are discussed under the following topics: (1) population, (2) health and nutrition, (3) housing and environment, (4) education and culture, (5) employment, working conditions, and social security, (6) social defense and welfare, and (7) income, consumption, and wealth. The author describes the availability of data needed to construct these indicators from government agencies and repeated surveys in India.

53. Raynauld, A. Social indicators: The need for a broader socioeconomic framework. Canadian Public Administration, 1975, 18, 99-103.

The author describes the general approach followed by the Economic Council of Canada in developing variables in models of various aspects of the social system. From the Council's point of view, society is seen as having the basic goals of well-being and equity; all other objectives are assumed to be contributory to these two primary goals. The social system is divided into various areas of concern, corresponding to existing institutional realities. The social indicator framework employed reflects the full array of outputs and related inputs for each area. The area of education is provided as an example of one of the ways in which the Council has approached the development of social indicators.

54. Terleckyj, N. E. Improvements in the quality of life: Estimates of possibilities in the United States, 1974-1983 (NPA Rep. No. 142). Washington, D.C.: National Planning Association, 1975.

This work represents "an attempt to devise an analytical framework for systematically assessing existing possibilities for social change measured by a set of quantitative indicators." In its focus on the quality of life, the analysis stresses outcomes rather than resources used. The dimensions of the quality of life are seen as goods in the sense that they are capable of satisfying human wants. Eighteen life quality dimensions are described and organized into six categories. Projections of 10-year trends are made for both the conditions measured by the indicators and the resource use associated with each dimension. Fixed versus discretionary activities and resources are distinguished, and contingent projections are made on their basis. Discretionary activities, their cost and their effect on the indicators within each dimension, are identified, and a 10-year projection of the resources available for these activities (by two subperiods and by public and private components) is made. Finally, within each dimension, the maximum feasible output of combinations of discretionary activities that can be undertaken within the estimated resource supply is calculated.

55. Wilcox, L. D. Social indicators and the measurement of social development in the third world: Constraints and potentialities, 1975. (ERIC No. ED 123 139)

This study discusses the relevance of social indicators for usage by less developed countries, examines the contexts in both the less and more developed countries with which social indicator methodologies must be compatible, and proposes a functional theory of society and societal development that offers a meaningful approach to social indicator construction. The method used was to test the theory and feasibility of social indicator methodologies by drawing general guidelines of how to measure the political, economic, social, cultural, and technical contexts of a given society, allowing for specific country variation. An examination of the implications of "functional theories" for conceptualization and measurement of social development is presented along with a brief description of society and its interrelated parts. The author states that due to the particular level of social development and cultural conditions characteristic of most less-developed countries, social indicator approaches originating in the more developed countries are more feasible. A limitation to the effectiveness of social indicators such as are discussed in this paper is that unless there is reasonable potential for the institutionalization of social indicators in the context of Third World development, the indicator's role is likely to be restricted to serving academic research rather than aiding the guidance of national development. (ERIC)

56. Bunge, M., and Sucre, M. G. Differentiation, participation, and cohesion. Quality and Quantity, 1976, 10(2), 171-178.

The authors propose two measures, one of social differentiation and one of social cohesion, that are applicable to any social system, whether an entire society or a subsystem of it. Both measures depend exclusively on the social structure of the system (that is, on the distribution of the population among the society's various niches) and can be computed from data filed in the census bureaus of most countries. On the basis of their measures, the authors conclude that the basis of spontaneous social cohesion is moderate participation; society disintegrates if everybody participates in everything or if participation falls below a certain threshold.

57. Chester, R. Official statistics and family sociology. Journal of Marriage and the Family, 1976, 38, 117-126.

  The author rebuts the ethnomethodological dismissal of the use of official statistics in sociological research. Although there are limitations to the official statistics available to researchers in the area of marriage and the family, these limitations do not derive from the official statistics being based on subjective interpretations, as claimed by some ethnomethodological writers. The limitations, rather, are a function of the categories of classification that are relevant to the work of the agencies involved. Sociologists cannot expect that their desires will govern the recordkeeping of agencies, although agencies often do respond positively to requests and suggestions from investigators. The author concludes that official statistics are usually highly reliable and serve as a sound foundation for sociological research.

58. Commission on Critical Choices for Americans. Qualities of life: Critical choices for Americans (Vol. 7). Lexington, Massachusetts: Lexington Books, 1976.

  This volume is a collection of 18 essays on topics relevant to current interest in quality of life. The first group of essays is concerned with the definition and characterization of the quality of life concept. Some of the topics considered are (1) classical and modern conceptions of "the good life," (2) the role of religion in quality of life, (3) the dependence of a group's concept of life quality on its socioeconomic status, and (4) the problems of measuring quality of life. The second group of essays deals with specific personal and policy choices that can directly affect quality of life. Examples of these choices include those concerned with (1) the structure of the social security system, (2) the consumer credit system, (3) the public media, (4) current practices in medicine and biology, and (5) city architecture. A common theme found in these essays is that most of the factors that can affect well-being do not have to draw heavily on either monetary or environmental resources.

59. Dever, G. E. A. An epidemiological model for health policy analysis. Social Indicators Research, 1976, 2, 453-466.

  The author argues that health programs that have desired to use health-related data in program planning have often failed because they have lacked a rational framework for data analysis. On the one hand, a cursory analysis of present disease patterns reveals chronic conditions for which the present system of organized health care has no immediate cures. On the other hand, infectious diseases of decades past have been all but eliminated by vaccines and antibiotics. Thus, before being able either to prevent or to arrest current disease processes as a result of health planning activities, the health field must be organized into more manageable elements. An epidemiological model that supports health policy analysis is presented, and four primary divisions of the model are identified: (1) system of health care organization, (2) life style (self-created risks), (3) environment, and (4) human biology. An application of the epidemiological model involves four steps: (1) select diseases that are of high risk and that contribute substantially to the overall morbidity and mortality; (2) proportionately allocate the contributing factors of the disease to the four elements of the epidemiological model; (3) proportionately allocate total health expenditures to the four elements of the epidemiological model; and (4) determine the difference in proportions between (2) and (3) above. Five tables illustrate how the epidemiological model is applied, showing the diseases selected for analysis, the contributing factors of each disease to the four components of the epidemiological model, the distribution of federal outlays for medical and health-related activities by category, the distribution of federal outlays of health expenditures by category, and a comparison of federal health expenditures to the allocation of mortality in accordance with the epidemiological model. The conclusion to be drawn from this study is that, based on current procedures for reducing mortality and morbidity, little or no change in present disease patterns will be accomplished unless there are dramatic shifts in present health policies.

60. Fagnani, F., and Dumenil, G. Health indicators or health system analysis? Extracts from a French survey. Social Indicators Research, 1976, 3(1), 37-74.

The conclusions of a French study devoted to the problem of health indicators are summarized in this article. After a review of statistical data available in France in the field of health and medicine, the theoretical problems linked with the meanings of the concepts of "need," "morbidity," and "state of health" are examined. A system analysis of this sector is proposed as a formal framework for interpretation of data in a unique quantitative health index, which seems preferable to the authors to the different essays on aggregation. Four types of indicators are proposed for monitoring as components of this health index: (1) exposure indicators, (2) morbidity indicators, (3) protection indicators, and (4) result or outcome indicators. The authors caution that the illustrative table of indicators of each of these types that they present is only a first approach, both because of the lack of suitable data in France and because of the weakness of the theoretical analyses made to date.

61. Fishburn, P. C. Evaluative comparisons of distributions of a social variable: Basic issues and criteria. Social Indicators Research, 1976, 3, 143-179.

A social variable can be understood as an attribute or characteristic of individuals' lives that is presumed to be related to their general well-being. These attributes can reflect aspects of physical or mental health, availability of educational or employment opportunities, actual education achieved, employment, economic income, freedom from fear of political repression, living conditions, and so forth. A distribution of a social variable over a population is understood as a function that assigns a level or value of the variable to each person in the population. Evaluative comparisons of distributions of the variable occur when some distributions are judged to be more conducive to social well-being than others, or when some distributions are judged to be better than others from the viewpoint of an individual. In this article, the meaningfulness of social and individual preference/value judgments for a social variable in isolation from other aspects of a social system is discussed from a systems perspective. The independence conditions that give meaning to such judgments are made explicit, and criteria that relate social preferences to the preferences of the individuals in the population (e.g., Pareto principles and related variants) are examined. Aspects of the social ordering relations that arise from these criteria are discussed (along with the compatibility or incompatibility of various criteria) and formalized in four lemmas, one theorem, and one corollary to the theorem.

62. Fitzsimmons, S. J., and Lavey, W. G. Social economic accounts system (SEAS): Toward a comprehensive, community-level assessment procedure. Social Indicators Research, 1976, 2, 389-452.

While much of the research on social and economic indicators has focused on the national level, this article presents a comprehensive community-level social economic accounts system (SEAS). The system is designed to enable social scientists, program developers, and public policy officials to better understand the effects of various types of public actions and policies upon the quality of life of individuals, the relative social position of groups of people, and the social well-being of the community. In order to be useful for diverse purposes, such as development of community theory, program evaluation, and policy formulation, the SEAS has the following characteristics: (1) it is community-wide, covering most aspects of community life that may influence or be influenced by public investment projects; (2) it is systematic in its approach to causal factors behind the patterns of stability and change in key variables; (3) it is sensitive to those distinguishing features of communities that indicate special needs and that can affect the operation and success of public projects; (4) it is applicable to time series analyses that are used to record and evaluate change; and (5) it is oriented toward the comparison of communities engaged in similar projects or that receive similar services and to other communities and norms. Data are specified for 15 sectors of community life: education, economic base, health, employment and income, welfare, government operations and services, law and justice, environment, social services, recreation and leisure, housing and neighborhood, transportation, communication, religious life, and family life). Data elements are organized under three generic sets of items: state variables (i.e., data describing the lives of people in the community), system variables (i.e., data describing the operations of institutions that affect people's lives), and relevant condition variables (i.e., data describing "system external" variables that have an effect upon the state and system characteristics). More than 400 items are included in the SEAS.

63. Garn, H. A. Models for indicator development: A framework for policy analysis. Washington, D.C.: Urban Institute, 1976. (ERIC No. ED 123 780)

This document summarizes aspects of a current approach to social indicator research and related problems in policy analysis generated by an interest in isolating major sources of variability in the generation of human welfare and developing indicators associated with welfare-generating processes. A set of models being developed for indicator research is described, and some of their implications explored. Suggestions are made for assessing performance from both an institutional perspective and a social perspective. The first section considers sources of variability in welfare generation that can be traced to the processes of transforming resources into welfare outcomes through production or consumption activities. The second section discusses extending the models to include sources of variability arising from the institutional settings in which these activities occur. The third section illustrates implications of these models for identifying the information requirements of the client and service providers of a prototypical public school system. (ERIC)

64. Harwood, P. de L. Quality of life: Ascriptive and testimonial conceptualizations. Social Indicators Research, 1976, 3, 471-496.

This article attempts to ascertain conceptualizations of quality of life (QOL) in the public mind and the priorities attached to various QOL components. Two approaches were taken, and the results were compared. Ascriptive, testimonial, and importance models were used, and a multidimensional scaling strategy was employed to compare dimensions obtained from respondents to (1) an ascriptive model comprising social, economic, and political dimensions (Economic Council of Canada, 1971) and (2) a representative testimonial model (Dalkey et al., 1972). (An ascriptive QOL model is one that is determined by experts or policymakers, while a testimonial model is based on individuals' perceptions of their well-being.) Results indicated a three-dimensional structure in the ascriptive case (education-communication-financial resources) and a unidimensional structure (comfort) in the testimonial case. Comparing the factor and scaling structures of both the ascriptive and testimonial models, the author concludes that items comprising political and economic factors are basic to a conceptual understanding of QOL. The QOL areas of health and freedom consistently showed the highest priority. Thus, the findings were consistent with those of other important studies.

65. Newfield, J. W., and Duet, C. P. Implications of quality of life for goal setting tasks of curriculum workers. Education, 1976, 97(2), 126-135.

The authors identify a trend in the social sciences toward providing the public with information that can be used for a variety of policy determination tasks. The term "social indicators" is used to describe various characteristics intended for these social reports. Indexes of quality of life, a popular media description of some social indicators, represent a multidisciplinary summary of characteristics people value. As such, they offer a unique resource to the curriculum worker concerned with the task of goal identification. As an example of the use of this resource, a survey of characteristics listed in quality of life indexes was made. This list was then compared with the goals of American education as formulated by several major commissions. In general, most of the traditional aims of education were reiterated in the indexes, indicating that quality of life indexes are a potentially useful resource for the curriculum worker. Some possibilities for new directions in aims of education are proposed. (PSYCH ABS)

66. Siegmann, A. E. Classification of sociomedical health indicators: Perspectives for health administrators and health planners. International Journal of Health Services, 1976, 6(3), 521-538.

The conceptualization and operationalization of health status measures are discussed. Traditional health indicators are noted, and a classification scheme is devised for sociomedical health status indicators. The application of sociomedical health status indicators is addressed. Health indicators are conceived as a subset of social indicators and, as any social indicator, are viewed as derivative from social issues. Interrelationships between different frames of reference for defining and measuring health, accompanying distinct health problem patterns in the United States, are examined from a developmental perspective. These patterns include infectious and communicable disease patterns, chronic degenerative diseases of aging and acute nonlethal disease patterns, and health problems and patterns associated with an individual's lifestyle. Mortality and morbidity rates, identified as traditional health indicators, are not considered to be adequate for the assessment of health status in developed countries. Taking into consideration the deficiencies of mortality and morbidity rates, a classification scheme for sociomedical health status indicators is developed that relates health definition frames of reference, measures of health status, and health problems. The role of sociomedical indicators in the formulation of health status measures is assessed. (NTIS)

67. Strumpel, B. (Ed.). Economic means for social needs: Social indicators of well-being and discontent. Ann Arbor, Michigan: University of Michigan Survey Research Center, 1976.

This book is concerned with the human conflict between needs and means, between material wants and lack of resources to satisfy them. Looking both at individuals and at some segments of society, the authors measure economic well-being and define its objective and psychological bases, its dimensions, and its relationship to economic incentives. In the introduction, an operational model of the interactions is presented as a conceptual framework. The articles in the book report on results of investigation in areas of research and development that have emerged from the model. Section I includes five papers that examine the sources and measurement of economic well-being. Their titles are (1) Economic Life Styles, Values, and Subjective Welfare; (2) Well-Being, Goals, and Motivation for Economic Advancement; (3) Persistence of Belief in Personal Financial Progress; (4) Effects of Social-Psychological Factors on Subjective Economic Welfare; and (5) Personal Efficacy and the Ideology of Individual Responsibility. Papers in Section II explore the use of indicators of economic well-being as performance criteria and as components for an early warning system of individual maladjustment and social conflict.

Titles of these papers are (6) Economic Well-Being as a Criterion for Performance: A Survey in Bulgaria and Greece; (7) The Quality of Consumption; (8) Economic Deprivation and Societal Discontent; (9) Factors Affecting Social Change; and (10) Responses to Economic Adversity: An Agenda for Research in a Changed Environment. (ERIC)

68. Blakely, E. J., Schutz, H., and Harvey, P. Public marketing: A suggested policy planning paradigm for community development in the city. Social Indicators Research, 1977, 4(2), 163-184.

This paper suggests that a public marketing model based on marketing principles can provide a potential framework for incorporating existing community development approaches into a strategy that relates to the current demands on cities for public accountability. At the same time, this model can provide city officials with a rational framework for determining the value of public goods and services to guide the allocation of resources between public and private consumption. Basic components of the public marketing model include (1) resource attraction, (2) resource allocation, and (3) persuasion. Public marketing tools that can be utilized for community development include (1) communications, (2) channels of distribution, (3) pricing, (4) product policy, and (5) marketing research. The authors argue that the public marketing model can supply insights into the operation of the community. More importantly, they suggest that the tools provided by the model can assist the community in determining and implementing the goals of its constituents. An example of a public marketing approach used in community development is briefly reviewed.

69. Fitzsimmons, S. J., and Lavey, W. G. Community: Toward an integration of research, theory, evaluation, and public policy considerations. Social Indicators Research, 1977, 4(1), 25-66.

This article presents a paradigm for the analysis of communities and investments designed to improve them. Its fundamental objective is to provide the researcher, the theoretician, the evaluator, and the public policymaker with a common analytic framework. If direct and indirect effects of investment programs (e.g., in education, economic development, and health) are documented longitudinally, the community can be analyzed as an independent, dependent, or mediating variable. The basis of this subsystem approach to studying communities in social science and policy theory consists of five concepts. They are (1) status, (2) change, (3) interaction, (4) duality of interaction and change, and (5) viability. An overview of these concepts, the objectives that are related to them, and the investment (or other intervention) evaluation questions of the paradigm is presented. Also, the types of analyses that this approach to community study can lead to are summarized. The definitions and procedures described in this article can be usefully considered in relation to an earlier paper by these same authors (Fitzsimmons and Lavey, 1976).

70. Gilmartin, K. J., Rossi, R. J., and Russ-Eft, D. F. Program impact evaluation paradigm for VISTA. Palo Alto, California: American Institutes for Research, 1977.

This is one of the volumes created in a project to provide evaluation models for the full-time domestic volunteer programs sponsored by the ACTION agency. A set of concepts is presented, defined, and used to provide a "common yardstick" for all of the various services and activities that VISTA sponsors or supports. The index of program impact selected was the constituency strength of a VISTA community, that is, the extent to which the communities affected by VISTA programs engage in self-directing behaviors. Investment behavior (behavior involving the expending of personal resources for expected positive return) and opportunity (the perceived costs of investments relative to expected returns) were key components of this index. A comprehensive list of indicators for the relevant variables is supplied.

71. Hubert, J. J. Bibliometric models for journal productivity. Social Indicators Research, 1977, 4(4), 441-473.

Bibliometrics is the collection of statistical methods that are applicable to various media of communication. Bibliometric models, for example, have often been used to characterize the productivity of professional journals. This paper presents a detailed chronological survey of these models and summarizes their usefulness. One common notation is used, derivation and proofs are in a statistical framework, and new relationships are illustrated. A list of relevant papers is provided, and those that have used these models are examined.

72. Mack, R. P. Comprehensive values and public policy. In K. Finsterbusch and C. P. Wolf (Eds.), Methodology of social impact assessment (CDS/32). Stroudsburg, Pennsylvania: Dowden, Hutchinson, and Ross, 1977.

While acknowledging that social indicators aim to measure levels of well-being, the author argues that there is a lack of information concerning how these levels are to be increased. The author attempts to use the conceptual apparatus available to economists to define a "micromodel" for individual total well-being that is relevant to the macro notions of societal well-being. A taxonomy of human needs and wants is presented, and the "consumer unit" is characterized as aiming to enhance a "vector" made up of these needs and wants. An exploratory model is presented that describes key elements for the consumer unit's efforts to optimize this vector. Three examples of policy problems set in terms of the exploratory model are presented, and the general implications of the analysis and some of its problems are discussed.

73. McIntosh, W. A., Klonglan, G. E., and Wilcox, L. D. Theoretical issues and social indicators: A societal process approach. Policy Sciences, 1977, 8(3), 245-267.

Well-being involves various levels: the individual, the institutional-distributive, and the societal. These levels are interrelated. Social indicators of well-being must be theoretically based in such a way as to take into account these levels. A societal process model is proposed to describe the levels of society and the nature of well-being at each level. Example social indicators are provided regarding the output and distribution of well-being, the effect of policy manipulable and nonmanipulable inputs, and the secondary consequences of inputs. The author suggests four benefits of using a societal process model. (1) The state of the nation in the fullest sense could be monitored and assessed. (2) The effects of certain changes in the societal environment could be traced through the entire system, in order to ascertain the type and degree of change and adjustment necessary for the nation to readjust to the new environmental conditions. (3) A societal process model would allow one to ascertain the short- and long-term effects of major societal policies on the individuals, institutions, values, and physical environment of a nation. (4) Intersectorial policymaking and planning would be facilitated if a societal process model were fully operationalized and in use.

74. Young, R. C. Social indicators for developing countries: A new approach. Ithaca, New York: Cornell University Department of Rural Sociology, 1977. (ERIC No. ED 137 025)

Designed to be self-contained, the material in this workbook on social indicators can be used for teaching and research purposes by agency field workers and undergraduates from developing nations who do not have a social science background. Originally presented to 22 professional people from Bangladesh, Indonesia, and the Philippines as part of a 10-week workshop on research methods for rural development held at the East-West Center in Honolulu, Hawaii (November 1975), this material includes many illustrative tables. Since data indicate food is virtually all that rural poor people in developing nations have and since most social indicator measures are more appropriate for urban dwellers in developed countries, it is suggested that food be made the core measure at the family, village, and national level. It is further suggested that food is inherently distributive (even the rich can only eat so much) and that, as an indicator of human welfare, food avoids the problem of value judgments upon the relative quality of life provided by a given technological innovation. (ERIC)

METHODOLOGICAL APPROACHES
TO CONSTRUCTING SOCIAL INDICATORS

1. Abrams, M. Social indicators and social equity. New Society, 1972, 22(529), 454-455.

   The author describes a "second wave of thinking" about social indicators that resulted in the development of subjective as well as objective measures of the quality of life. A 1971 survey is described that involved 600 respondents who represented the total population aged 16 years and older in the seven conurbations in Britain. The survey form asked respondents to rate their levels of satisfaction/ dissatisfaction in twelve domains: (1) housing, (2) neighborhood, (3) democratic process, (4) standard of living, (5) being a housewife, (6) job, (7) leisure, (8) health, (9) marriage, (10) family life, (11) religion, and (12) education. Results showed that respondents' ratings of their present and expected quality of life fell short of what they felt the quality of their lives should be ideally. The author does not claim that this experiment in developing subjective measures of the quality of life is without weaknesses, but he does conclude that, for many people, perceptions of the quality of life will not be notably raised without political and financial measures that satisfy their standards of social equity.

2. Baster, N. (Ed.) Measuring development: The role and adequacy of development indicators. London: Frank Cass, 1972.

   This volume is a collection of papers that first appeared in a special issue of the Journal of Development Studies (April 1972). The papers address the following topics: (1) the nature of development indicators, (2) the methodology of welfare measurement, (3) economic criteria for human development, (4) procedures for the selection and validation of development indicators, and (5) the notion of political development.

3. Bush, J. W., Fanshel, S., and Chen, M. M. Analysis of a tuberculin testing program using a health status index. Socio-Economic and Planning Sciences, 1972, 6, 49-68.

   The authors define an index of health status and an index of function status. Each member of a target population belongs to one of several levels of function, from complete well-being (valued 1.0), through various levels of dysfunction (with intermediate values), to death (valued 0.0). The utility numbers assigned between 0 and 1 to the levels of function are called function weights. The distribution of a population among the various levels over time is considered to be a stochastic process where group prognoses make up the transition probability matrices. Using a set of function weights, the function status of a person or population can be computed for each point in time. The output of a social program (i.e., the expected difference between the two function-histories with or without the program) is measured in units that are independent of disease form, permitting comparisons among health programs for different diseases. To illustrate the uses of these two indexes in health planning, a countywide tuberculin testing program is evaluated. The results are subjected to a sensitivity analysis by recomputing the effectiveness of the program using several arbitrary sets of weights, demonstrating that program output is dependent on value judgments about relative levels of function. The use of this procedure for decisionmaking is discussed.

4. Drewnowski, J. Social indicators and welfare measurement: Remarks on methodology. Journal of Developmental Studies, 1972, 8(4), 77-90.

The author claims that only three distinct aspects of social conditions can be considered measurable: demography, social relations, and welfare; each of these aspects must be measured in its own way. This paper is concerned with the methodology of measuring welfare by means of objective indicators. Four kinds of welfare indicators are distinguished: (1) flow of welfare (level of living) indicators, (2) state of welfare indicators, (3) welfare effect indicators, and (4) productivity effect indicators. Specific features (direction, scaling, and distribution) required for welfare indicators are discussed. The author describes the role of value judgments in welfare measurement and presents the pros and cons of developing aggregate indices for measuring the flow and state of welfare.

5. Firestone, J. M. The development of social indicators from content analysis of social documents. Policy Sciences, 1972, 3(2), 249-263.

The author distinguishes his conception of social indicators (that they should be indicators of theoretically central concepts) from the view held by Marcus Olson and others (that social indicators should be indicators of normatively central concepts). Five types of theoretical concepts that social indicators should assess are presented. These include (1) the physical movements of goods, services, and communications viewed from a social exchange or directed action perspective (i.e., transactions); (2) the noncultural products of past transactions that provide part of the context of ongoing transactions; (3) the documentary products of past transactions, art, film, media records, literary products, political communications, and other documents that provide another portion of the context of transactions; (4) the relational configuration of psychological states of individual members of a social system; and (5) the physical characteristics related to transactions (e.g., land use patterns, climate). Five data types are associated with each of these theoretical concepts: (1) interview response data, (2) institutional records, (3) artifactual data, (4) simple observation, and (5) contrived observation. The author shows that little effort has been made to use artifactual data to assess cultural products and group psychological states. A review of the literature is summarized that suggests sizable crosstemporal correlations may be found between indicators of national motives derived from content analysis of school texts and various national social (condition) indicators. The author argues that researchers should turn away from survey research as a tool for generalizing analyses of society. Instead, more effort should be made to analyze literature, art, film, songs, and so on in developing social indicators.

6. Gitter, A. G., and Mostofsky, D. I. Toward a social indicator of health. Social Science and Medicine, 1972, 6, 205-209.

This paper presents an approach toward aggregating individual health variables and outlines six steps involved in creating a composite social indicator of health status. These steps include (1) systematic examination and selection of existing statistical data on health in the United States, (2) designation of a base year for these data, (3) factor analysis of the data using the factor loadings of the variables from the base year as weights, (4) selection of factor scores for the 50 states for use as national indicators, (5) computation of a weighted sum of each state's factor scores, with weights determined by the amount of variance that the particular factor accounted for, and (6) computation of the mean of all summed factor scores to represent the national indicator of health. Three research examples are presented to illustrate some of the various types of analyses that could be performed with the proposed indicators. The authors point out that both the use of factor analysis and the procedure suggested for summing scores of selected factors represent only one possible approach to index construction. They note that questions concerning the stability of the relationships among variables over time and the completeness of the components that are selected for reflecting overall health status remain to be answered.

7. Little, D. Social indicators, policy analysis, and simulation. Futures, the Journal of Forecasting and Planning, 1972, 4(3), 220-231.

This article suggests that simulation models would serve as useful tools for developing and using social indicators in the policy-making process. One such model (STAPOL) is described, and current and future applications for this type of simulation are discussed. (ERIC)

8. Seminar on Social Indicators. Social indicators: Proceedings of a seminar. Ottawa: The Canadian Council on Social Development, 1972.

This volume is a collection of ten papers, with reports on discussions and workshops. Opening papers and their discussion center on two opposing views of "what to do next" insofar as the development of social indicators is concerned. The first paper urges determined, consistent, and constant effort to develop statistical time series. In contrast, the second paper urges that a moratorium on indicator development be imposed until several basic questions regarding the purpose and scope of the social indicator movement are more clearly defined and understood. Other papers report preliminary results on the development of livability indicators, habitability indicators, and indicators of conditions in the Canadian North that can be used to assess the effects, both intended and unintended, of government policies and programs. A summary report on current work and on future plans of Statistics Canada is presented. The monograph concludes with brief summary reports from individuals involved in four workshops. These workshops were concerned with technical problems, welfare indicators, philosophical problems, and urban indicators. Discussion agendas for each of the workshops, biographical notes on the contributors, and the conference schedule are included in the report.

9. Wachs, M., and Kumagai, T. G. Physical accessibility as a social indicator. Los Angeles: University of California School of Architecture and Urban Planning, 1972. (NTIS No. PB-212-740)

A discussion is presented of the ways in which accessibility to employment and urban services constitutes an important measure of the quality of urban living and how accessibility might, therefore, be included as an important component of a social report for a city or region. A conceptual framework is presented for measuring accessibility in terms of the ease with which citizens may reach a variety of opportunities for employment and services. This framework, which could be used to evaluate transportation and regional plans, differs from current approaches based upon travel volumes and travel times. The use of the proposed measures of accessibility is illustrated with data on accessibility to employment and health care facilities in Los Angeles, and these data are interpreted to illustrate differences as a function of location and socioeconomic status.

10. Wilcox, L. D. Social and economic indicators of rural development from a sociological viewpoint: A suggested empirical approach. Ames, Iowa: Iowa Agricultural and Home Economics Experiment Station, 1972. (ERIC No. ED 084 076)

An empirical approach to the development of a system of social indicators is suggested in this paper. The paper also suggests a more inductive approach to social indicator research, with three methodological phases representing increasing levels of methodological sophistication. The first steps attempt to conceptualize social indicators that reflect the human meaning of societal change and development by examination of the life experience of nonmetropolitan people. Second, attempts are made to work inductively toward the macro-level, by combining these empirical indicators into more abstract indicators that provide multidimensional profiles of individuals and subgroups. Third, attempts are made to develop relational models of community systems and to draw causal inferences by the use of controlled indicators designed to measure the social effects of major demographic changes as one strategic force in societal change. (ERIC)

11. Clark, T. N. Community social indicators: From analytical models to policy applications. Urban Affairs Quarterly, 1973, 9, 3-36.

Two types of social indicators are distinguished: descriptive and analytical. The essential characteristic of analytic indicators is that they are integrated into models and are, therefore, useful for understanding patterns of association and change. Both types of indicator can be evaluated in terms of three criteria: (1) measurability, (2) social importance and shared goals, and (3) policy importance. At the community level, these criteria are used to suggest a more intensive focus on (1) policy outputs, the products of collective decisions, in terms of (a) fiscal and (b) performance indicators and (2) policy impacts, the changes brought about in a society as a consequence of policy outputs. Problems that may be encountered in measuring policy outputs and impacts are discussed. A model is derived to explain variations in common expenditures of municipalities (policy outputs) based on data from 51 cities. The author suggests that the model serve as a "core model" to which specific variables might be added if policy changes concerning them are being considered. It is noted that policy impacts are less well understood than policy outputs. A methodology is presented for assessing attitudes toward public policies that may help in evaluating these impacts.

12. Gitter, A. G., and Fishman, J. E. Social indicators of educational opportunity. (CRC Report No. 68). Boston: Boston University Communication Research Center, 1973.

The authors developed two types of factor analytical social indicators--factor scores and basic variables--which were shown to apply in aggregating multivariate education data. State indicators of educational input and educational output for 1960 were computed. They were used as dependent measures in analyses of variance and covariance, with region, density, urbanization, percent of whites, personal income, and nonwhite migration as independent variables. The relationships between social indicators of educational input and output were tested, both with and without controlling for the context of the relationships. Procedures for computing both state and national indicators for a base year and any subsequent years are described. (PSYCH ABS)

13. Hughes, B., and Volgy, T. On the difficult business of conducting empirical research in a data-poor area. American Journal of Political Science, 1973, 17, 394-406.

In answering criticisms (Kenneth S. Hempel, "Comparative Research on Eastern Europe: A Critique of Hughes and Volgy's 'Distance in Foreign Policy Behavior,'" American Journal of Political Science, 1973, 17, 367-393) of an earlier essay (B. Hughes and T. Volgy, "Distance in Foreign Policy Behavior: A Comparative Study of Eastern Europe," Midwest Journal of Political Science, 1970, 14, 459-492), the authors point out that the concept of distance in foreign policy behavior was operationalized in several ways because analysis of the concept disclosed that more than a single measurement strategy was necessary. The validity of the indicators that were used in the original study is discussed, and the authors defend both their aim to describe rather than to explain foreign policy behavior and their decision not to weight components of the distance indicators. They also describe and argue in support of the "common variance" validity technique they employed. The article concludes with a restatement of the study's objectives, all of which were accomplished. These objectives were (1) to see if quantitative methods could be usefully applied to a data-poor area (i.e., where information is not readily available); (2) to see if a general concept that was related to other foreign policy concepts customarily applied to Eastern Europe could be constructed; and (3) to probe for patterns of external behavior with the objective of systematically describing events.

14. Maloney, J. F. (Chair). Progress in development of social indicators. Symposium presented at the Twenty-Eighth Annual Conference on Public Opinion Research. Public Opinion Quarterly, 1973, 37(3), 423-487.

These papers were presented: N. Zill and R. Parke, Social Science Research Council, Center for Coordination of Research on Social Indicators; "From Self-Report to Social Report: Uses of Survey Data in Social Indicators"--the social indicators' potential of existing survey and poll archives has yet to be adequately exploited, and therefore the SSRC Center for Coordination of Research on Social Indicators is working to improve the utilization of survey data. J. P. Robinson, Survey Research Center, University of Michigan; "On the Correspondence between Subjective and Objective Social Indicators"--several hypotheses were discussed to explain the lack of correspondence often found between people's subjective evaluation of their quality of life and their objective behaviors. J. R. Goeke, Opinion Research Corporation; "Three Decades of Experience with Social Indicators: Are They Useful in Forecasting?"--six classes of indicators were discussed that have been very predictive but are largely ignored.

15. Olkinuora, E. On the problems of developing education indicators. Acta Sociologica, 1973, 16, 284-302.

This article examines the problems that can arise in the development of educational indicator systems. The work is based on a review of the social indicators literature and on the author's personal involvement in a project to develop educational indicators at the Institute for Educational Research, University of Jyvaskyla, Finland. The problems that are discussed concern (1) development of a frame of reference for indicator selection, (2) operationalization of variables, (3) construction of indicators, and (4) political considerations involved in the selection and use of particular indicators. A preliminary frame of reference is presented that integrates quantitative and qualitative educational inputs and outputs with (1) educational equality, (2) educational relevance from the societal perspective, (3) educational relevance from the individual's perspective, and (4) educational efficiency. Problems of operationalizing goals within this framework are illustrated, and the inadequacies of existing education-related data for addressing the suggested goals are enumerated. The implications of educational indicators for policy-making are discussed from both the "optimistic" view that indicators can provide educational information more concisely and the "pessimistic" view that indicators will not influence policymaking any more than other education-related data because policymakers rely largely on political considerations in formulating educational policy.

16. Andrews, F. M. Social indicators of perceived life quality. Social Indicators Research, 1974, 1(3), 279-299.

Several of the possible weaknesses associated with perceptual indicators are addressed in some detail in this article. New research evidence and certain philosophical perspectives are presented, and the author concludes that none of these weaknesses is sufficient to invalidate the development and use of perceptual indicators. Several questions are presented that must be answered in order to generate the basic knowledge on which to build an adequate series of indicators of perceived well-being. These questions range from "What are the concerns of a given group of people?" and "How do concerns relevant to perceived well-being relate to one another?" to "How stable are these individuals' evaluations of particular concerns?" and "What are the costs and difficulties of collecting perceptual measures from these people?" The author suggests that the methods he and his coworkers have used make it possible to answer these questions for adult Americans and for major subgroups within the United States population and may make it possible to answer these questions for individuals in other cultures.

17. Andrews, F. M., and Withey, S. B. Developing measures of perceived life quality: Results from several national surveys. <u>Social Indicators Research</u>, 1974, <u>1</u>, 1-26.

This article reports on the status of a series of studies oriented toward the assessment of perceived life quality. A conceptual model is presented that considers a person's overall sense of life quality to be understandable as a combination of affective responses to life "domains," which are of two types--role situations and values. More than 100 items that were used to measure a wide variety of domains and 28 items assessing perceived overall life quality are presented. (Various subsets of these items were used in interviews with several representative samples of American adults.) The domain items are grouped into a smaller number of semi-independent clusters that were found to be internally stable across ten different subgroups of respondents and whose interrelationships were found to be highly replicable in independent national samples. The results of a series of analyses, several of which were replicated in more than one survey, are presented. It was found that (1) an additive combination of 12 selected domains explained 50%-60% of the variance in an index of overall life quality; (2) neither other domains nor several social characteristics variables contributed additional explanatory power; (3) this level of explanation was achieved in each of 22 subgroups of the population; and (4) additive combinations of domains worked as well as more complicated combinations.

18. Beardsley, P. L., Kovenock, D. M., and Reynolds, W. C. Measuring public opinion on national priorities: A report on a pilot study. <u>Sage Professional Papers in American Politics</u>, 1974, <u>2</u> (Series No. 04-014).

U.S. National Income Accounts data were used in this paper as a point of departure for developing 15 spending categories for use in hypothetical allocation of all funds available to the public sector. The aim was to develop an instrument and related procedures that could be used to assess public opinion regarding national priorities. The 15 categories were presented twice to approximately 225 persons, who were asked either to allocate markers (representing pennies making up the "tax dollar") according to their perceived priorities or to redistribute markers and allocate new markers in accordance with these perceptions. (A new measurement strategy had to be developed in this case because existing strategies were available for assessing local priorities only.) Reliability and validity coefficients were calculated, and the measurement strategy was deemed both to be content-valid and to have considerable reliability and construct validity.

19. Carmichael, N., and Parke, R. Information services for social indicators research. Special Libraries, 1974, 65, 209-215.

   This article gives examples of the resources available for social indicators research and describes the activities of the Social Science Research Council's Center for Coordination of Research on Social Indicators in meeting the information needs in this field. (ERIC)

20. Chen, M. M., Bush, J. W., and Patrick, D. L. Social indicators for health planning and policy analysis. San Diego, Calif.: University of California, 1974. (NTIS No. PB-250 610 3ST)

   The concept of health involves two dimensions: the level of function at a point in time and the probability of transition to other levels at future times. The paper describes two proposed indices derived from this concept that describe different aspects of community-wide health status and provide useful information for health policy decisions. The proposed function status index can be constructed using current data collection mechanisms and would significantly augment our knowledge of the level of well-being of the population. The other proposed index, value-adjusted life expectancy, would give a reasonable approximation of an ideal health status index, but would require collecting new kinds of data. This index would indicate physical and mental health status, would incorporate both value and prognostic dimensions, and could be used for estimating the output and contribution of health programs to the health status of the total population. (NTIS)

21. Espenshade, T. J. Estimating the cost of children and some results from urban United States. Social Indicators Research, 1974, 1, 359-381.

   The testing of economic theories of fertility has been hampered by the absence of suitable data on the direct (versus opportunity) costs of children. This study intends to help remedy this deficiency by proposing a new method of estimating the magnitude of money expenditures parents make on their children. This method is then applied to the urban sample of the 1960-61 United States Consumer Expenditure Survey to estimate the total money expenditure costs of children to age eighteen. The distribution of these costs by income level, by birth order, by age of the child, and by components of cost (food, housing, clothing, and so on) is considered. There were three principal findings. (1) The first child in a family is likely to be more expensive than subsequent children. The marginal cost of the first child ($37,000-$46,000 to age eighteen in 1961) is twice that of the second or third child ($17,000-$23,000). (2) Costs increase with the age of the child. A child between the ages of 12 and 17 costs approximately three times as much as one between ages 0 and 5.

(3) A family's standard of living declines (although real income is allowed to increase) until the eldest child reaches age eighteen, then starts to rise again. This decline is steeper and more prolonged the greater the number of children.

22. Fontane, P. E. Viability of congregation as a religious indicator. Social Indicators Research, 1974, 1(2), 243-255.

This article presents an indicator of the "health" of a religious congregation, termed the Viability of Congregation (VOC), which was applied and, in the author's view, was found to be reliable, valid, and cognitively simple. This indicator is obtained by determining the number of active statuses (behaviors that contribute to the meeting of community expectations of the particular congregation) existing in the congregation during a period of time and the number of participants (congregation members). The indicator is considered to be complete when its reciprocal, nonparticipants per active status, is ascertained. Thus, the VOC is simply the number of active statuses per participant in a congregation compared to the number of active statuses per nonparticipant. In an effort to test the validity of the VOC indicator, information was used from a study of three midwestern Episcopal churches. The perceived effectiveness of each congregation was determined by applying Shippey's (1952) criteria for an effective urban church. The rankings of the churches based on the perceived effectiveness scale and the VOC indicator were the same. The author suggests that the VOC indicator would be applicable to assessing the viability of community groups other than the church and cautions that care must be exercised in interpreting the indicator since it carries no implications regarding the causes of stability or change in these groups.

23. Gordon, R. A., and Gleser, L. J. The estimation of the prevalence of delinquency: Two approaches and a correction of the literature. Journal of Mathematical Sociology, 1974, 3(2), 275-291.

This article proposes that the proportion of a cohort that have become delinquent by a given age, here called the prevalence of delinquency, is an important social indicator. Methods by which this index can be estimated from data are indicated, and errors in previous sex- and race-specific prevalence estimates published by T. P. Monahan (1960) for the city of Philadelphia are corrected. The differences between the sexes and between the races shown by these corrected prevalence estimates are of sufficient magnitude to render suspect any comparisons of prevalences of delinquency among cohorts that do not take account of the sex and race compositions of the cohorts to be compared. (PSYCH ABS)

24. Kogan, L. S., and Jenkins, S. Indicators of child health and welfare: Development of the DIPOV Index. New York: City University of New York Center for Social Research, 1974.

This study examines the relationships among 25 indicators of child health and welfare in 1960 and 1970 in order to develop a

Disorganized Poverty (DIPOV) Index applicable across several levels of aggregation. The authors analyzed relationships among these variables at three geographical-political levels: (1) the 62 community planning districts in New York City, (2) the 62 counties in New York State, and (3) the 50 states and the District of Columbia. They factor analyzed the variables at each of the three levels of aggregation, finding similar patterns across all three levels. The patterns were found to be stable between 1960 and 1970. The authors suggest that the DIPOV Index be seen as a first approximation toward the measurement of the "quality of child life."

25. Krug, R. E., and Jung, S. M. Systems for evaluating the impact of rural development programs. Washington, D.C.: American Institutes for Research, 1974.

This is the final report of a six-year project to develop techniques for assessing the behavioral outcomes of government-sponsored political, economic, and social action programs in rural Thailand. The primary index developed was the investment behavior of a village, that is, the extent to which the inhabitants of a village were investing their personal resources in the lawful opportunities for social, political, and economic improvement being made available by government programs. The report details the development of instruments, indicators, and observation procedures and presents the results obtained.

26. Liu, B. C. Quality of life indicators: A preliminary investigation. Social Indicators Research, 1974, 1(2), 187-208.

Concern over the quality of life in the United States seems to have increased proportionally with technological advancement and growth in material wealth. Growing public interest in social, economic, political, and environmental conditions has led to the search for indicators that adequately reflect the overall "health" of the nation and its citizens' well-being. This article develops a systematic methodology for assessing social, economic, political, and environmental indicators to reflect the quality of life in the United States. Nine indicators--individual status, individual equality, living conditions, agriculture, technology, economic status, education, health and welfare, and state and local governments--are compiled from more than 100 variables for 50 states and the District of Columbia. Primarily on the basis of 1970 data, QOL indexes are generalized and the states are rated. Comparisons among similar studies are made, and analyses among indicators are also performed. Regressing an overall social-economic-political-environmental measure of the quality of life and income rank on the nine composite indexes, the author reports that total variance in the overall index was mostly accounted for by the economic status indicator; by itself, it explained approximately 80% of the variance. Next in explanatory power to economic status were the equality indicators. When combined with the economic status indicator, they jointly explained approximately 90% of the variance. In contrast, the government and the individual status indicators showed very little explanatory power. The author points out that these findings suggest that quality of life can be appreciably enriched if efforts are dedicated to enhancing economic status and individual equality in the United States.

27. Rummel, R. J. Quarterly technical report number 5: July 1, 1974--September 30, 1974 (Report on the Dimensionality of Nations Project). Honolulu: Hawaii University Department of Political Science, 1974. (NTIS No. AD/A-006 817/1ST)

A set of indicators of national social structures and their behavior was screened from previous results, and data on them were prepared for a variety of analytical studies. The linkages between structural indicators and behavioral indicators were then determined using canonical analysis. Considerable effort went into preparing a set of chapters on conflict theory for the principal investigator's manuscript on "The Sociological Field and Conflict." (NTIS)

28. Strumpel, B. (Ed.). Subjective elements of well-being: The OECD Social Indicator Development Programme. Papers presented at a seminar of the Organisation for Economic Co-operation and Development, Paris, 1972. Washington, D.C.: OECD Publications Center, 1974. (ERIC No. ED 110 371)

This volume resulted from an attempt to compile comprehensive and accurate data about the popular reaction to social change for a seminar attended by European and American social scientists. The volume contains eight papers that reflect the three objectives of the seminar: (1) a review of psychological indicators of social change; (2) an exploration of new areas of survey measurement of psychological phenomena; and (3) a mapping of research priorities. The first paper contrasts social indicators of the subjective type with the customary hard statistics and identifies areas for the development of indicators. The next paper stresses that quality implies value judgment and that experience is anchored in individual notions of adequacy. The relationship between subjective and objective indicators is the topic of the next paper, which points to the role of the social environment as a source of subjective welfare. Various measurement and methodological questions are dealt with, in particular the issues of scale development and causal modeling of satisfaction structures. A report on the substantive research in the area of economic welfare is followed by a caution against a straightforward interpretation of satisfaction measures as indicators of well-being. Finally, two papers deal with the interaction between the individual and society from two different perspectives. The volume concludes with a summary of the seminar proceedings. (ERIC)

29. Utah Water Resources Laboratory. Water resources planning, social goals, and indicators: Methodological development and empirical test. Logan, Utah: Author, 1974. (NTIS No. PB-242 025/5ST)

A methodology for comprehensive evaluation of water resources development and use (TECHCOM) has been developed and partially field tested. A model of three societal goals consists of nine primary goals successively articulated into increasingly specific subgoals. Achievement of subgoals is perceived as affected by measurable social indicators whose values are perturbed by water resources actions. Linking the elements of the goal taxonomy by connectives results in an evaluation system. Historical, political, and philosophical considerations of the proposed system are discussed in Part I. Part II describes the results of the Rio Grande of New Mexico test including public perception and weighting of the subgoals and goals and development of specific connectives. Future values of 128 social indicators for five action plans for four five-year intervals to 1987 are estimated using a computerized system based on an inversion of an input-output model interacting with social and environmental indicator connectives. (NTIS)

30. Ziller, R. C. Self-other orientations and quality of life. Social Indicators Research, 1974, 1(3), 301-327.

This article presents a theory, related measures, and a series that offer a new approach to the study of quality of life. The approach is phenomenological; that is, evaluations of the quality of life are taken to be a function of individual experience. To facilitate the experiencer's communication, a nonverbal technique of measuring the personal meaning of events and environments is employed. The approach involves the development of indicators of the meaning of events and environments as experienced in the relationship of the self and significant other persons. Crucial features of the approach include (1) emphasis on personal meaning; (2) comparison of the personal meaning of such events as love, marriage, parenthood, and work; and (3) search for a wide range of meaningful personal experience. A series of studies are described that emerge from this framework dealing with alienation; gain or loss of social status; love, marriage, and parenthood; and transitional states. The author is engaged in applying this methodology to the study of drug abuse programs, work incentive programs, and first grade classes in a particular school system.

31. Abt, C. C. The social costs of cancer. Social Indicators Research, 1975, 2, 175-190.

The annual social costs of cancer, exclusive of economic costs such as medical costs and loss of earnings while incapacitated, are systematically developed in this article. Some twenty-five separate social costs are identified from a review of the oncology literature. Social costs to the victims of cancer, to the immediate family and colleagues of the victims, and to caregivers are included. These social costs are translated into equivalent money costs on the basis of market prices and opportunity costs of the behaviors devoted to obtaining a desired product or end-state. The total social costs are computed by multiplying the average individual total social costs by the number of such individuals affected. The social costs of cancer are found, by this approach, to exceed the simple economic costs of the disease by more than an order of magnitude. Evidence is also presented indicating that some forms of cancer incur much higher social costs than others, as well as much higher social costs than economic costs. This suggests that a more optimal allocation of public resources for reducing the total costs of the disease would shift resources to alleviation of social costs where investment in medical therapies approaches saturation. The sum total of the minimum annual social costs of cancer is estimated at $2.5 billion or about $7,000 per victim if death-related costs are excluded. Including these costs, the annual social cost of cancer is estimated at $138 billion or about $40,000 per victim. This figure represents approximately 10% of the United States Gross National Product.

32. Barrows, R. L., and Shaffer, R. E. Indicators of development in Wisconsin counties: 1970. Social Indicators Research, 1975, 2, 333-360.

This article focuses on the problems involved in measuring economic and social development. Existing theories of economic and social change are used to select important indicators of development. For each indicator, principal components analysis is used to collapse several related variables into a single index. The indexes are labeled economic base, economic growth, personal economic opportunity, health inputs, health status, educational inputs, and educational attainment. The selection of variables on these indexes and construction of the indexes themselves was constrained by two factors: (1) the data had to be available from existing data sources, and (2) the selection of the indicators and the procedure used to form indexes had to be easily understandable, inexpensive, and quickly repeatable by state or local agency personnel. The indexes are found to be consistent with one another, and the variables entered into the indexes with the expected sign. On the basis of the high intercorrelation found among the indexes, the authors suggested that they may measure development. Since there is no rigorous or absolute measure of development against which the authors could check the validity of the indexes, they relied upon the opinions of persons with experience in measuring development. State agency staff and local development groups that had used the indexes considered them to be reasonable development measures.

33. Bennett, K. F., and Blackburn, R. T. Social indicators of institutional commitment. Journal of Industrial Teacher Education, 1975, 13, 48-52.

The paper describes how five indicators were developed to measure the comparative degree of commitment of a group of community colleges to their vocational-technical areas. The criteria of a "good" measure are developed, the findings of a pilot study are displayed, the indicators are critiqued, and alternatives are suggested.

34. Brenner, B. Quality of affect and self-evaluated happiness. Social Indicators Research, 1975, 2, 315-331.

The author uses the concept of "quality of affect" to develop variables that describe how a person is feeling. The extent of marked positive affect, the extent of marked negative affect, and the modal hedonic level or modal quality of affect are presented as three components of a quality-of-affect measure. Alternative two-component measures are also developed. These measures and those asking respondents to evaluate how happy they are were administered to a sample of adults in Washington County, Maryland. Findings from this study indicate that self-evaluated happiness has a strong positive relationship with quality of affect. Furthermore, each quality of affect component was found to be associated with self-evaluated happiness when the other two components were held constant. While the quality-of-affect measures were designed to give equal weight to positive affect and negative affect, self-evaluated happiness was found to be related more strongly to positive affect than to negative affect. The author suggests that quality of affect and self-evaluation happiness measures should both be included in surveys aimed at assessing quality of life.

35. Colley, D. G. A social change index--An objective means to discern and measure the relative current social condition of cities, towns, and their sub-communities. Social Indicators Research, 1975, 2, 93-118.

This article presents a social change index that was developed in response to a social planning need. The aim of planners was to assess social pathology of communities on an objective basis. The index is derived from a combination of social indicators that are reported by census tract in Rhode Island on an annual basis. The index, which does not include census data, is considered particularly sensitive during the interdecennial years. High mobility rates, particularly in central cities (up to 80% in some areas of these cities), cause census data for these years to be unrepresentative in many instances. The author suggests that the index may also be used for priority ranking of need for social program services, program monitoring, and program evaluation. Rhode Island is expected to institute a Committee on Social Statistics among whose primary responsibilities will be to encourage state agencies to publish their social statistics by census tracts in their annual reports. It is presumed, consequently, that a larger number of current social indicators will be available to be included in the social change index and increase its accuracy. Indicators that are presently included in the social change index are (1) born out of wedlock rate per thousand females in age group 15-44; (2) death rate per thousand population; (3) hepatitis rate per ten thousand population; (4) low birth weight infants rate; and (4) the ratio of the total number of persons in the age group 0-14 and the number of persons in the age group 65+ to the number of persons in the age group 15-64 (dependency ratio).

36. Deichsel, A., and Stone, P. J. Newspaper headlines: A multinational content analysis project on textual indicators from mass media. Social Science Information, 1975, 14(1), 112-116.

Representatives of ten countries participating in the Pisa Workshop expressed interest in starting a project to investigate the development of social indicators based on the contents of the mass media. The proposal is still preliminary; this report is intended to announce the proposed project and to invite others to participate. Some of the issues to be studied include (1) the relative amounts of attention to local, regional, national, and international events, (2) the specificity of treatment, (3) the patterns of attention to continuing events, (4) the impressions created concerning actors and events by the way they are described, (5) whether the press can be clustered on the basis of content analysis, and (6) whether symbol changes in the international press can be monitored and compared. Participants considered focusing on newspaper headlines. The authors discuss the advantages and disadvantages of using headlines without analyzing the accompanying text.

37. de Neufville, J. Social indicators and public policy: Interactive processes of design and application. New York: Elsevier North Holland, 1975.

This book, which deals with quantitative measures and their role in public decisionmaking, addresses the questions of how to design indicators that can be useful to policy and how to design processes to make better use of such information. Case material is used to identify the problems confronting those who wish to design, use, or evaluate indicators for public decisions. Specifically discussed are the role of quantitative measures in problem definition, the setting and context for projected systems of indicator production and use in United States statistical policy, the problems and constraints on creating concepts, the criteria for choosing among data collection processes and recognizing how they may change concepts, choices for structuring data and their implications, ways of institutionalizing indicator production and creating public acceptance, and the range of uses and the effects of letting data become manipulable for short-term political considerations. (NTIS)

38. Dignan, G. Youth-Community Coordination Project: Research results and organization for planning-- Tacoma, Washington. Washington, D.C.: American Public Welfare Association, 1975. (ERIC No. ED 131 159)

In March 1975, the American Public Welfare Association's Youth-Community Coordination Project (Y-CCP) began to develop a coordinated youth services system in Tacoma/Pierce County (and four other sites around the country), funded by National Discretionary LEAA funds from the National Institute for Juvenile Justice and Delinquency Prevention. The Y-CCP developed a local data base to facilitate the coordinated planning process. A social area analysis identified three kinds of census tracts in the city after analysis of 33 social indicators from 1970 census data. A youth needs assessment was administered to 1,109 youth from grades seven to twelve in Tacoma public schools. A community resources questionnaire was distributed to youth-serving agencies. A follow-up survey was distributed to 42 of those agencies to obtain a measure of their perception of youth needs that could be compared to the youth perspective, and gaps in services were identified. A systems development survey was conducted with administration of key statutory agencies in the city. In addition, the Y-CCP stimulated coordination activities using the data as an organizing tool. The Youth Concerns Committee was identified as the most realistic starting place for planning efforts. Membership was increased, and 25 appropriate representatives of various service clusters were selected. (ERIC)

39. Doyle, J. G. Social statistics for the elderly: Area Level System, Stage I: Omaha. Washington, D.C.: Administration on Aging, 1975. (NTIS No. PB-259 788/8ST)

Potential sources of data for a system of social statistics on the aged in Omaha, Nebraska are identified, and the feasibility of developing such a system on an areawide basis is investigated. Conducted by the Census Use Study under contract with the Administration on Aging, the investigation is one of several directed toward the development of social statistics systems based on the following principles: the use of secondary (existing) data; the use of small area data; the use of data in time series; and the distillation of data into summary statistics. The report of the Omaha Standard Metropolitan Statistical Area (SMSA) demonstration project includes a detailed description of the data inventory process, presentation of the data uncovered to date and a discussion of their usefulness, and a discussion of the costs and staffing requirements of several options for development of a social statistics system in Omaha. Based on the conclusion that such a system is feasible, a series of steps for its implementation is outlined. These steps include negotiating access to existing data, making arrangements for copying necessary files, and processing the data; distilling the data into a set of composite or summary statistics; analyzing the final data set and developing a social report for the Omaha area; developing a user's manual; and providing for system update. (NTIS)

40. Hill, R. B. Using social statistics for policy and program development. Urban League Review, 1975, 1(1), 8-11.

Issues such as income, occupations, affirmative action, family structure, social class, and poverty are discussed in terms of their appropriate assessment to develop social policies and programs. Methodological biases, such as making generalizations about groups on unrepresentative samples, are discussed. (ERIC)

41. House, P., Livingston, R., and Swinburn, C. Monitoring mankind: The search for quality. Behavioral Science, 1975, 20(1), 57-67.

This paper describes an effort by the Environmental Studies of the Environmental Protection Agency to develop a methodology for the assessment and quantification of the term "quality of life" (QOL). An experiment was performed at an EPA-sponsored QOL conference held in 1971. The 150 attendees were asked to reach a consensus on a list of QOL factors; the result was 47 factors organized in three areas: political/social, economic, and environmental. These factors were then weighted by the participants in the hope of providing a useful tool for the decisionmaking process. Given the sponsorship of the conference, the fact that the environmental area contained the most factors and received the most weight may not be representative of the views of the general population. Discussion of the exercise points out the problems and pitfalls to be avoided in trying to quantify the concept. The authors suggest that measuring QOL as a happiness function may not be feasible, and they suggest that a dissatisfaction index with threshold values on each factor may be more useful. A brief description of the dissatisfaction index is presented with some current applications.

42. Inhaber, H. Philosophy and limitations of environmental indices. Social Indicators Research, 1975, 2(1), 39-51.

    This article is based on the author's work in developing an environmental quality index for Canada. It considers some of the major problems faced in creating environmental indices. The problems that are discussed include (1) the incompleteness of environmental data (e.g., only measures of airport visibility go back as far as 20 years); (2) the difficulty involved in setting environmental standards; (3) the lack of a consistent geographical basis for data (e.g., some water quality measures are available by province--a political division--while others are in terms of particular watersheds); (4) the lack of timely data (e.g., air quality information in terms of specific pollutants is often one year out of date); (5) the weighting of subindices; and (6) the lack of a one-to-one correspondence between effluent and ambient measures. A diagram of the data that were collected and how they were arranged into indices and subindices is presented.

43. Liu, B. C. Quality of life indicators in the U.S. metropolitan areas. Kansas City, Mo.: Midwest Research Institute, 1975.

    The empirical results of a 1970 study designed to assess the quality of life in 243 metropolitan areas are provided in this booklet. The quality of life components include 123 variables related to overall economic, political, environmental, health and education, and social conditions. The booklet is divided into five sections that explain the quality of life components and provide the results from large, medium, and small metropolitan areas across the country. The final section offers concluding remarks. The results indicate that the west coast, east north-central, mountain, and New England regions had relatively more metropolitan areas with outstanding or excellent quality-of-life ratings. In contrast, the southern states showed a relatively larger number of low-rated metropolitan areas, although they do have several areas with high ratings. The most outstanding large metropolitan areas were in the Pacific and northern regions, while the most outstanding middle-sized metropolitan areas were in the east and north-central regions. The most outstanding small metropolitan areas were in the east north-central region. (ERIC)

44. Milbrath, L. W., and Sahr, R. C. Perceptions of environmental quality. Social Indicators Research, 1975, 1, 397-438.

    This paper aims to offer a conceptual and operational definition of perceived environmental quality. Four subenvironments are viewed as constitutive of any human environment: (1) the natural environment, (2) the environment of the dwelling, (3) the activity environment, and (4) the characteristics of the community. Two scales are proposed to assess the perceived quality of each environment, a valence scale and an importance scale. An instrument was developed and tested in two counties in New York state. It was concluded that those persons who are highly satisfied with their environments are (1) more likely to have a high regard for technology, (2) more likely to have little or no concern about environmental problems, and (3) more likely to favor economic growth.

45. Peskin, H. M. Accounting for the environment: A progress report. Social Indicators Research, 1975, 2, 191-210.

This article reviews the progress of a project to introduce imputed values of environmental services into the national accounts. A brief discussion of the project's relation to the social measurement research underway at the National Bureau of Economic Research leads to a statement of the accounting principles that are used. These principles rely on the imputation of money values to two types of input and output flows that arise when any sector of the economy chooses to employ the services of the environment. The fundamental aim of these accounting principles is to set the value of this input flow equal to the least cost society would bear were the producer denied the use of the environmental service. The term "cost" refers to all losses suffered by society as the producer is denied access to the environmental asset and thus is forced to substitute other valuable resources for the free environmental services he or she had been receiving. The social cost of this resource shift is thus reflected in the costs of pollution control equipment, changes in production process, reductions in the level of production, alterations in product characteristics, or some combination of these factors. Preliminary accounting data, the results of a study of the distribution of air pollution damage (which relied on these data), and a brief discussion of the policy and research implications suggested by these preliminary results are presented. The article concludes with a technical appendix that demonstrates that a sector's contribution to air pollution emissions may be a poor indicator of its contribution to social damage.

46. Riedel, M. Perceived circumstances, inferences of intent, and judgments of offense seriousness. Journal of Criminal Law and Criminology, 1975, 66(2), 201-208.

The author discusses the Sellin-Wolfgang index of delinquency as a potential social indicator and as an empirical referent of theoretical terms. Respondents had little difficulty inferring intent from the perceived circumstances, and there was little support for the Jones and Davis theory that different circumstances would lead to different degrees of willingness to attribute intent. Results indicate that in assessing the seriousness of criminal events, perceivers make only unimportant inferences as to whether the offender intended the act. This suggests that external aspects of the event, such as the amount of injury, theft, or damage, is all that the respondent needs to make a reliable assessment of social injury. (PSYCH ABS)

47. Rodgers, W. L., and Converse, P. E. Measures of the perceived overall quality of life. Social Indicators Research, 1975, 2, 127-152.

This article describes a study to construct measures of the perceived quality of life. Respondents participating in the national study were asked to assess satisfaction or dissatisfaction with each of a set of fifteen domains of their lives. They were also asked to describe their lives as a whole, using both satisfaction and semantic-differential types of scales. Canonical correlation analysis is used to find the combinations of domain-specific and global items with the highest correlation. The two indices derived from this analysis, the

Index of Well-being and the Index of Domain Satisfactions, are examined in relation to a variety of demographic and situational variables, including age, indicators of socioeconomic status, employment status, and size of community. The relationships discovered provide evidence for the validity of these indices. The reliability of the measures (as measured cross-sectionally) and their stability over a period of some eight months are both acceptably high. The authors conclude that both of these measures form acceptable indicators of the perceived overall quality of life.

48. Schmid, A. A. Systematic choice among multiple outputs of public projects without prices. <u>Social</u> <u>Indicators</u> <u>Research</u>, 1975, <u>2</u>, 275-286.

Cost-benefit analysis has been applied to the evaluation of public investment projects whose outputs have market derived prices. When prices are attached to all inputs and outputs, it is possible to systematically rank projects by net return and to derive some implications for budget size. A consistent and explicit basis for ranking projects with nonpriced outputs has been lacking, however. In this article, a step-by-step procedure is developed for systematic choice when some or all outputs have no market value reference points. The seven steps in the method are (1) define output categories, (2) determine importance weights, (3) standardize importance weights, (4) determine project outputs, (5) compute utilities, (6) construct cost-benefit ratios, and (7) compute implied prices. An appendix addresses problems that may be encountered in working through these steps. These problems include (1) uncertainty regarding the occurrence of outputs; (2) differences among regional and group preferences; (3) differences among mixed market and nonmarket related outputs; and (4) differences among the relations between mixed market and nonmarket related outputs and inputs. The method makes clear the information that can be provided by the analyst and that which must be provided by the political process. The procedure gives no easy answer to value conflicts among members of society, but it does allow citizens to determine if public officials are making project choices consistent with announced objectives and explicit value weights. Such procedures could facilitate public participation in project choice and monitoring the behavior of public officials.

49. Southern California Association of Governments, Social Indicators Group. <u>Guide</u> <u>to</u> <u>social</u> <u>indicators</u> <u>for</u> <u>local</u> <u>government</u>, <u>or</u> <u>how</u> <u>to</u> <u>improve</u> <u>your</u> <u>policy</u> <u>decisions</u> <u>with</u> <u>information</u> <u>you</u> <u>didn't</u> <u>even</u> <u>know</u> <u>you</u> <u>had</u>. Los Angeles: Author, 1975. (NTIS No. SHR-0000843)

The document is designed to provide local decisionmakers and their technical staff with an insight into the use of statistics as social indicators. Social indicators are defined as statistics about the conditions of society that facilitate social policy choices. These statistics are developed to provide a concise and direct quantitative measure of each condition. The use of social indicators is illustrated in two areas of local decisionmaking, estimation of community needs and the allocation of resources. Examples describe the development of social indicators to help select target areas for three particular programs: child care centers, mental health funds allocation, and senior citizen nutrition programs. Ten steps in the social indicator development and use process are detailed. It is emphasized that social indicators are not substitutes for the political process, that social indicators are not used to accumulate data about individuals, and that program evaluation cannot be accomplished with social indicators. (NTIS)

50. Stolte-Heiskanen, V. Family needs and societal institutions: Potential empirical linkage mechanisms. Journal of Marriage and the Family, 1975, 37, 903-916.

This article considers family needs and institutionalized mechanisms linking societal inputs to these needs as potential concepts for the analysis of the interrelationships between the family and society. Two fundamental input-output linkages that are described concern (1) reproduction of labor power and (2) the ideological perpetuation of the society. These linkages are related on the family level to four universal reproductive functions: (1) biological, (2) economic, (3) social, and (4) spiritual. Needs customarily associated with these functions are also considered. Data from 24 European countries are used to examine whether social indicators can be developed to assess family needs and societal inputs aimed at ameliorating these needs. The countries are classified as either "highly industrialized" or "developing industrialized" and as having either high or low levels of "familism." Indices of "family needs" and "family welfare" are developed, and the relationship among these indices is explored. Results suggest that most of the countries fall into two groups: "high family welfare-high family needs" and "low family welfare-low family needs."

51. Taylor, D. G., Aday, L. A., and Anderson, R. Social indicator of access to medical care. Journal of Health and Social Behavior, 1975, 16(1), 39-49.

A social indicator of access to medical care, known as the symptoms-response ratio, is introduced. The indicator reflects the difference between the number of visits in response to symptoms that actually occur and the number of visits a panel of physicians feel is appropriate for the same symptoms. The symptoms-response ratio uses a checklist of symptoms administered to all persons or their proxies over one year of age in the 1970 Center for Health Administration Studies nationwide survey. For each of 22 symptoms on the checklist, people were asked whether they experienced the symptoms during the survey year and, if a symptom was reported, whether a physician was contacted about it. A panel of 40 physicians was asked to estimate, based on their training and experience, what percentage of people in a particular age group with a specific symptom should see a physician for it. Empirical data are provided on the reliability of physician estimates and on the value of the symptoms-response ratio itself for a national sample of the U.S. population. Findings on the symptoms-response index for various race, residence, income, and regular-source-of-care subgroups affirm differentials in access that are generally thought to exist in terms of other access indicators. The value of access indicators such as the symptoms-response ratio is that they incorporate an explicit external norm of medical appropriateness against which a population's actual responses to perceived symptoms of illness may be compared. Nonwhites, rural farm people, and those who have no local place to go for medical care were found to have less access to care than judged appropriate. The index also suggested "overutilization" among certain groups. (NTIS)

52. Allardt, E. Dimensions of welfare in the Comparative Scandinavian Study. Acta Sociologica, 1976, 19, 227-239.

The Comparative Scandinavian Study made two basic distinctions: welfare versus happiness and level of living versus quality of life. Welfare is based on needs: the amount of welfare is defined by the degree of need-satisfaction. Happiness, on the other hand, refers to subjective perceptions and experiences: the amount of happiness is defined by the extent to which people feel they are happy. The level of living concept refers to material and impersonal resources with which individuals can master and command their living conditions. Quality of life, on the other hand, refers to the satisfaction of love and self-actualization that depends on how a person relates to other people, society, and nature. These two distinctions are used to construct a two-by-two table of areas in which assessments can be made, all of which have been referred to as "quality of life" on occasion in the past. In the Comparative Scandinavian Study in 1972, all four cells were operationalized and measured using national probability samples of approximately 1,000 15-to-64-year-olds from each of four countries: Denmark, Finland, Norway, and Sweden. The material level of living and people's satisfactions were found to be independent of each other, and only weak relationships were found between objective level of welfare and attitudes of dissatisfaction.

53. Andrews, F. M., and Crandall, R. The validity of measures of self-reported well-being. Social Indicators Research, 1976, 3(1), 1-19.

Using a new analytic approach, construct validity estimates were developed for proposed social indicators of self-reported well-being. Two separate investigations are reported: the first involved data on six aspects of well-being each assessed by six methods from 222 adults in one geographic area; the second, a partial replication and extension, involved a more limited set of indicators measured on a sample of 1,297 respondents representative of all American adults. The results provide evidence that perceptions of well-being can be measured by single questionnaire or interview items using any of four formats with validities in the range of 0.7 to 0.8 (implying that roughly half to two-thirds of the variance is valid) and with correlated method effects contributing less than 10% of the total variance. Two other formats, however, were markedly less valid. These findings are important in view of past criticisms of "subjective" social indicators as lacking in validity, and the findings can guide current efforts to develop new ways to assess the quality of life. Methodologically, the article illustrates the feasibility and utility of deriving parameter estimates of structural equation models of multimethod-multitrait data using Joreskog's LISREL algorithm. The possibility of deriving validity estimates in this way, even when the data include correlated errors, opens new and important opportunities to precisely assess the amount of error variance in much social science data.

Methodological Approaches (MA)

54. Andrews, F. M., and Withey, S. B. Social indicators of well-being. New York: Plenum Press, 1976.

This is a study about perceptions of well-being. Its purpose is to investigate how these perceptions are organized in the minds of different groups of American adults, to find valid and efficient ways of measuring these perceptions, to suggest ways these measurement methods could be implemented to yield a series of social indicators, and to provide some initial information about the levels of well-being perceived by Americans. The findings are based on data from more than five thousand Americans and include results from four separate representative samplings of the American population. The book is organized into three major parts, which are preceded by a general introduction and followed by a series of appendixes. Part 1 describes the methodological and conceptual explorations that provide the fundamental knowledge base on which one can begin to build a series of perceptual indicators. Topics that are covered include identifying and mapping areas of concern, measuring global well-being, predicting global well-being, evaluating the measures, and exploring the dynamics of evaluation. Part 2 examines a large number of perceptual indicators and what they tell about the well-being of the American population and 27 major subgroups defined on the basis of sex, age, race, socioeconomic status, and stage in the family life cycle. Both specific concerns and overall perceptions of well-being are discussed. Part 3 is concerned with the application of the development efforts and is addressed to those who would use the indicators, or modifications of them, to assess perceived well-being in future investigations.

55. Biderman, A. D., and Drury, T. F. (Eds.). Measuring work quality for social reporting. New York: John Wiley & Sons, 1976.

In 1973, the Bureau of Social Science Research established a working group on indicators of the quality of employment. The objectives of the working group were to clarify a variety of conceptual, methodological, and organizational issues regarding how our national statistical systems might more adequately monitor the quality of employment. Each member of the group prepared a paper on an assigned topic; these 13 papers form this volume. The papers are divided into four categories: (1) fundamental perspectives; (2) health, satisfaction, well-being, and human development; (3) labor market processes, income, and economic justice; and (4) system orientations of workers and systemic characteristics of work.

56. Campbell, A., Converse, P. E., and Rodgers, W. L. The quality of American life. New York: Russell Sage Foundation, 1976.

An earlier Russell Sage Foundation publication, Indicators of Social Change (Sheldon and Moore, 1968), had reviewed the structural and institutional changes in American life. The present book is viewed as a companion piece that explores the development of indicators to document the subjective quality of life in this country. The analyses in the volume are based on a national sample survey of 2,100 persons, with a follow-up of a subset of the respondents eight months later. Topics include indicators of a general sense of well-being;

domains of life experience; satisfaction, aspirations, and expectations; residential environment; work; marriage and family life; women; and black people.

57. Chen, M. K. A comprehensive population health index based on mortality and disability data. Social Indicators Research, 1976, 3, 257-271.

In this article, two versions of a new population health index based on the mortality and disability experiences of nations or communities are proposed for comparing their overall health status. One version is the ratio of the mean mortality rate of selected population groups to the mean disability-free rate of survivors. The other version is a composite of these variables, transformed to stabilize their variances, which are so weighted as to maximize the probability of correctly differentiating "healthy" and "unhealthy" nations. While the first version is easier to compute and to interpret, the author suggests that it may not be the best index for differentiating countries known to be "healthy" and "unhealthy." One drawback of the measure is that the health state of the living, as indicated by the rate of disability, has considerably less effect than does mortality on the measure until the former becomes substantial. The second version is considered to be a more valid way of summarizing mortality and disability data. Impressive results are reported for this version with hypothetical data.

58. Clark, T. N. (Ed.) Citizen preferences and urban public policy: Models, measures, uses. Beverly Hills, California: Sage Publications, 1976.

This collection of papers originally appeared as a special issue of Policy and Politics (1976, 4(4)). The papers address general questions regarding the measurement of citizen preference, the testing of median preference theories, the problem of survey format, and the potential uses of survey data in policymaking.

59. DeWeese, L. C. Computer content analysis of printed matter: A limited feasibility study. Public Opinion Quarterly, 1976, 40(1), 92-100.

The author attempts to determine how a limited study of computerized content analysis of printed media could (1) identify and anticipate emerging public interests and (2) measure the importance and rate of change of public interest in these issues. The long-range objective is to develop quantitative indicators of changing social values. It is concluded that an ongoing, large-scale system of computer content analysis of media, appropriate for social indicator development, is technologically feasible but expensive. Such an analysis offers a complementary method to public opinion survey research for the study of changing public issues. (PSYCH ABS)

Methodological Approaches (MA)

60. Harvey, A. S., and MacDonald, W. S. Time diaries and time data for extension of economic accounts. Social Indicators Research, 1976, 3(1), 21-35.

The present contents of Canadian economic accounts are described, as are critcisms of income and product accounts and some recommended modifications. Types of nonmarket activity that should be added to economic accounts are listed; these consist of (1) household operations (food growing, meal preparation, care of house and clothes, and marketing and record keeping), (2) household maintenance (repair, upkeep, and home improvement), (3) family and child care, (4) education and training, (5) volunteer work, (6) travel to and from work, and (7) leisure. The significance of each of these nonmarket activities for measuring the investment of human capital and the overall welfare of society is described, and previous attempts at measuring these activities are reviewed. The authors present criteria for evaluating any methodology for collecting time allocation data for extension of economic accounts. The three basic approaches to collecting time allocation data (interviews using standard instruments, interviews using time diaries, and observational techniques) are compared and contrasted in terms of the previously discussed criteria. The authors recommend the use of time diaries over the other two approaches.

61. Katz, S., and Akpom, C. A. Measure of primary sociobiological functions. International Journal of Health Services, 1976, 6(3), 493-508.

The index of independence in activities of daily living (ADL) is described as a scale whose grades reflect profiles of the behavioral levels of sociobiological functions. Six sociobiological functions are delineated, including bathing, dressing, toileting, transfer, continence, and feeding. The hierarchical structure of the index of ADL makes it possible to rank the overall functional status of people in an ordered manner, to make comparisons among them as individuals or groups, and to detect changes over time. Developmental studies encompassing children and adults, the mentally retarded, the physically disabled, and noninstitutionalized as well as institutionalized people are reported. In view of relationships between primitive societies and behavior and parallelisms between the order of index functions and patterns of child growth and development, the index of ADL appears to be based on functions of sociobiological primacy. This concept is supported by methodological and applied observations. The index has been used to generate predictive information about chronic conditions and to evaluate the benefits of long-term services. It has also been used in profiled measures of the severity of illness. As a screening measure and survey measure, ADL has provided information about health needs and outcomes of management, planning, policymaking, research, and teaching. (NTIS)

62. Khakhulina, L. A. An attempt at constructing social indicators for integrated study of rural development. Novosibirsk, Russia: USSR Academy of Sciences, 1976. (ERIC No. ED 133 099)

A system of social indicators for the integrated and systematic study of rural socioeconomic development was constructed. Specific features of the system were that it (1) embraced nearly all aspects of life activity of the rural population, ranging from work in the public sector to leisure behavior; (2) included social indicators that measured the lifestyle of rural dwellers, their qualitative characteristics, and some of their attitudes, as well as the conventional statistics assessing the functions of economic institutions and the distribution of population among social groups; and (3) relied on a systematic conceptual framework of socioeconomic development of rural communities. This paper describes the main stages in the system's development. Some methodological principles of devising systems of social indicators for integrative study of socioeconomic development of rural communities are discussed. Emphasizing the need to use scholars engaged in different rural studies as judges for the selection of necessary indicators, the paper presents two ways of constructing social indicators: empirical and theoretical. (ERIC)

63. King, D. C., and Long, C. J. Measuring the quality of life: Are we making progress? Intercom, 1976, 82, 3-16.

Perspective on the term "quality of life" is developed through reading and photographic selections, and ways of measuring life quality are suggested. Statistical tables offer comparative national and global data on indicators including population, literacy, nutrition, and government expenditures. (ERIC)

64. Lippman, L. Indicators of societal concern for mentally retarded persons. Social Indicators Research, 1976, 3, 181-215.

The author reports on an effort to develop and validate a set of indicators of societal concern for mentally retarded persons. Although the immediate applicability is at the level of the individual state (within the United States), the instrument is adaptable for comparison across nations as well as the discernment of trends over time. After the crucial first step of conceptualization, the task was to obtain consensual validation from a representative group of authorities. With a few exceptions, the respondents' reactions did validate the assumptions and value-orientations of the instrument. The instrument was reformulated on the basis of the respondents' comments. The outcome was a series of 105 items, grouped under eight headings: Living Arrangements; Economic Security; Health Services; Education; Social Services; Work; Legal Rights and Liberties; Government Services and Funding. The author claims that the instrument could easily be adapted for measuring a society's treatment of physically disabled and psychiatrically disturbed individuals and could be extended to measure the sensitivity and concern of a society for all those in the population who are dependent in any way (e.g., children and old people).

65. Nijkamp, P. Socio-economic and environmental indicators as determinants of interregional migration flows. Social Indicators Research, 1976, 3(1), 101-110.

In this paper, an explanatory model is formulated and is used to operationalize the proposed linkage between geographical mobility,

Methodological Approaches (MA)

socioeconomic conditions, and environmental characteristics. Two issues are given primary attention: (1) whether environmental factors can explain migration patterns and (2) whether there are historical shifts in the extent to which environmental factors explain migration rates. The analysis is illustrated by the results of a study on migration in the Netherlands.

66. Organization for Economic Co-operation and Development. Measuring social well-being. Paris: Author, 1976.

This report summarizes the effort of the OECD since 1973 to develop a comprehensive set of social indicators. The report is divided into five parts. Part I reviews the working methods and the approach of the OECD to indicator development. Part II describes the methodology used to specify indicators and the criteria used to select indicators and discusses how the data should be disaggregated. Part III lists areas of social concern and the indicators that have been proposed to assess conditions in these areas. Part IV summarizes the goals of the OECD social indicators project, and Part V reviews the generalizability of the approaches taken. Appendixes to the report present this list of social concerns and examine the availability of data required by the proposed indicators.

67. Rosenberg, B. Evaluation of the status and effectiveness of state and local human services information systems. Silver Spring, Maryland: Applied Management Sciences, 1976. (NTIS No. SHR 0001010)

The Social Indicators Project of the Center for Social Research and Development (CSRD), a division of the Denver Research Institute of the University of Denver, is described. The project was conducted by CSRD for DHEW and was designed to identify indicators of social problems and progress in social development at the county level; create a single data bank for gathering, storing, and analyzing data; identify relationships between socioeconomic conditions and social problems; and produce information useful for regional and state human service planning and evaluation. The primary goal of the project was to provide useful quantitative information about social, economic, and demographic conditions in DHEW Region VIII. The planning and development of the system is discussed, and the data base and data processing procedures are described. Among the activities conducted under the project were data collection analysis, development of a recommended data list based on a comprehensive list of social concerns, workshops and seminars to demonstrate the uses of social indicators at various levels, updating of the data base, special analyses based on system data, and technical assistance. Because the project is no longer operational, site visit observations were limited and information on the utility of the system was derived primarily from program documents. It is concluded that the system was well used within Region VIII, but that the use of system outputs outside the region was limited. User comments were favorable. Exhibits summarizing the Social Indicators Project data base and listing the publications of the Social Indicators Project are provided. A bibliography of available system documentation is included. (NTIS)

68. Rudd, N. M., and Kline, K. L. Money value of consumption and income of rural families: Two measures of economic status. Social Indicators Research, 1976, 3, 217-236.

   In this study, a measure of economic status, money value of consumption, is defined, and its relationship to income is examined using data collected from 628 United States rural families and 1,170 North Carolina rural families. Findings suggest that money value of consumption is linearly related to income for rural families, that the variance of money value of consumption is proportional to income, and that money value of consumption is more equally distributed than income. Money value of consumption is more closely related to income for one-person and four-or-more-person families than for two- or three-person families. A comparison of how the two measures (money value of consumption and income) rank rural families by consumption status indicates that income is most likely to rank families inaccurately at very low and very high levels of income. Since most researchers will probably have to continue to rely on some type of money income measure, the findings of this study may contribute to the understanding of the extent to which income errs as a proxy for money value of consumption and may, therefore, assist in the appropriate interpretation of income as a measure of economic status. The author suggests that researchers who intend to rely on income as a measure of economic status should supplement it is the following ways: (1) account for the value of home-produced food, fuel, income in the form of produce, and gifts received; (2) indicate ownership of durable goods and the level of savings and other assets held by the family; (3) account for the equity a family has in its housing and for the quality of that housing; and (4) account for farm operating expenses for families who operate their own farms.

69. Sweney, A. B., and Tubbs, V. A. Periodic factors involving reenlistment decisions: Measured by social indicators. Wichita, Kansas: Kansas State University Center for Human Appraisal, 1976. (NTIS No. AD-A043 229/4ST)

   A number of statistics available in most military posts were assessed on a monthly basis for a period of 48 months. These variables included areas that were perceived to have relevance for "quality of life," and the number of reenlistments after first and second terms were used as criterion variables. After being correlated through time using Cattell's "P-Technique," they were factored by principal components and rotated by Varimax to yield nine independent interpretable factors. These were identified as economic cycles, seasonal cycles, unit activity cycles, excessive training, holiday joy, declining strength and morale, second term reenlistments, Christmas prosperity vs. New Year's slump, and individual economic pressure. All of these factors were related to some degree to the first and second term reenlistments.

70. Bharadwaj, L., and Wilkening, E. A. The prediction of perceived well-being. Social Indicators Research, 1977, 4(4), 421-439.

   Regression analysis of data from a sample of Northwestern Wisconsin residents shows that a limited number of domain satisfactions accounts for a significant proportion of the variance in life satisfaction. Most life satisfaction is derived from domains that are personal, broader in scope, and central to the individual and that gain ascendency in the social and psychological life space of the individual as a result of differences in sex, age, and income. Satisfaction with health, family, and even community override work satisfaction as the main source of men's life satisfaction, while satisfaction with family life easily overwhelms other domain satisfactions as a predictor of the life satisfaction of women. Also, the effect of family satisfaction is much stronger for women than men and stronger during the socially and biologically most productive years of life than in maturity. The contribution of satisfaction with spare time activities, family, work, and so on to the life satisfaction of the elderly is consistent with a theory of reengagement in fewer but more meaningful roles. Income differences do not sharply discriminate among the predictors, except at the extremes. Perceived satisfaction in various domains accounted for only 20%-40% of the variance in overall life satisfaction; however, purely objective measures usually explain less than 10% of the variance in global measures of life satisfaction. Overall, the study demonstrates the efficacy of domain satisfaction measures as predictors of life satisfaction.

71. Blau, T. H. Quality of life, social indicators, and criteria of change. Professional Psychology, 1977, 8(4), 464-473.

The author discusses a variety of social, economic, and psychological approaches to operationalizing "quality of life," including ten scales as indicators of life quality of persons in psychotherapy. A proposal is offered for developing social indicators based on input from a consortium representing all constituencies, including consumers or mental patients themselves. The author suggests that the joint wisdom produced by this consortium could help forge policies efficacious for reversing today's deteriorating quality of life.

72. Buttel, F. H., Wilkening, E. A., and Martinson, O. B. Ideology and social indicators of the quality of life. Social Indicators Research, 1977, 4(3), 353-369.

This paper explores the possibility that social-psychological, evaluative measures of social well-being/quality of life perceptions may embody unintended ideological elements. The authors argue that individual quality of life satisfactions are likely caused, in part, by "satisfactions," or conservative orientations, vis-a-vis societal institutions. Four dependent measures of quality of life attitudes--overall life satisfaction, service satisfaction, community satisfaction, and powerlessness--are derived from factor analyses and established measurement procedures. Each of these quality of life indicators is found to exhibit significant bivariate associations with measures of political-economic ideology. These relationships are somewhat reduced, but persist at statistically significant levels, when sociodemographic background variables are held constant. The authors assume that researchers in the subjective social indicators field want to measure quality of life or well-being, not ideology. Therefore, they suggest that political-ideological indicators be incorporated into study designs and that these relationships be controlled for before asserting causal relationships.

73. Citrin, J. Political alienation as a social indicator: Attitudes and action. Social Indicators Research, 1977, 4(4), 381-419.

The author reviews the conceptual status of the most widely used measures of alienation and concludes that the distinctions among them reflect differences in the attitude object and in the format of the survey questions that make them up. Next, the paper reviews trends in attitudes toward American political institutions as reflected in national opinion surveys between 1964 and 1974, demonstrating that the decline in confidence in national leaders was only rarely accompanied by a repudiation of systemic values and processes. The main body of the paper reports on evidence about the relationship between political alienation and political action, drawn from surveys in the San Francisco Bay Area conducted by Berkeley's Survey Research Center in 1972 and 1973. A new Political Alienation Index is used as the attitude measure, and a model is developed to account for alienation's causal influence on participation in unconventional political protest. By the use of multiple regression analysis involving multiplicative terms, it is shown that political alienation interacts with the individual's cognitive and political skills, age, attitudes toward the protest act, and structural opportunities for action to promote protest behavior. Thus, the political relevance of rising disaffection with the ongoing order can only be assessed when other characteristics of the alienated and their political context have been established. The author concludes by calling on other researchers to undertake an inventory of behaviors that includes responses to public policy and acts of social responsibility as well as "conventional" and "unorthodox" participatory acts.

74. Dever, G. E. A. The pursuit of health. Social Indicators Research, 1977, 4(4), 475-497.

This paper contains a literature review relating health legislation to the cost of medical care. The author claims that health legislation has had the effect of increasing costs, but has done little to reduce disease rates. A death-coding system is presented that is based on the more global cause of death (e.g., lack of exercise, cigarette smoking) instead of the final disease (e.g., lung cancer). The author argues in favor of demoting the restorative and curative approaches to medicine and instead promoting the concept of preventive medicine. Three tables and ten figures depict the leading causes of death by number and rate for Georgia and for the United States, 1900-1973; infectious and chronic disease death rates, United States, 1900-1970; cycles of infectious and chronic disease patterns; health expenditures, United States, 1930-1975, per capita and percent of GNP; an epidemiological model for health policy analysis; and sample certificates of death.

Methodological Approaches (MA)

75. Evers, S., and McIntosh, W. A. Social indicators of human nutrition: Measures of nutritional status. Social Indicators Research, 1977, 4(2), 185-205.

The authors contend that the social indicators movement has neglected indicators of nutritional status. This report presents a discussion of the problems of validity, reliability and precision that plague current measures of nutritional status. Additional concerns for technically feasible and economically sound field methods are also expressed. Direct methods of collecting nutritional indicator data that are discussed include (1) dietary surveys, (2) anthropometry, (3) clinical assessment, (4) biochemical tests, and (5) surveys of age of menarche. Indirect methods of data collection that are considered include (1) analysis of vital statistics, (2) analysis of morbidity rates, and (3) monitoring of birth weights. Concepts, data, social indicators, and data sources for component measures of nutritional status that could be used to measure the distribution of nutritional status across subgroups are presented. The indicators considered include (1) dietary intake adequacy, (2) physical development, (3) age of menarche, (4) tissue level of nutrient, (5) child mortality by cause rates, (6) child-total population mortality ratio, (7) child morbidity by cause rates, and (8) average birth weight. In addition to nutritional status indicators, the authors suggest that descriptions of market conditions, familial and community social structure, and the place of food in local culture will provide information to deal with current deficiencies and descriptions of changes in these socioeconomic and cultural conditions will suggest further nutritional problems.

76. Greenbaum, W. Measuring educational progress: A study of the national assessment. New York: McGraw-Hill, 1977.

This book provides a comprehensive evaluation of the goals, objectives, and procedures of the National Assessment of Educational Progress (NAEP). Separate chapters discuss NAEP's objectives and organizational development; its division of knowledge into subject areas; the subject-area objectives; exercise development; measurement of background variables; the sampling design and the exercise packages; reporting of results; past and future uses of the assessment; and social indicators and the reform of education. Highly critical of some aspects of NAEP, the study is followed by a response from the staff of the National Assessment. (ERIC)

77. Jaeger, R. M. An abundance of answers in search of questions: On a methodology of assessment through indicators. New York: Annual Meeting of the American Educational Research Association, 1977. (ERIC No. ED 135 872)

Some observations are presented on a social indicators approach to statewide educational assessment. The context of the observations is the Oregon Department of Education model for educational planning. Much of what is said can also be applied to educational planning and program evaluation at the federal level or in large school systems. For the purposes of this discussion, a social indicator is defined as any statistical time series on a quantitative variable that is measurable and time-referenced. One-shot measures are excluded, as are sequences of qualitative descriptions. Operating from the premise that agencies may be forced to build educational indicators from extant data collections, some of the methodological problems inherent in this approach are discussed. Some possible solutions are proposed, both short-term and long-term, for measurement issues such as specifications bias, construct validity, and political validity. Possible areas for research and experimentation leading to more ideal sets of educational indicators are described. (ERIC)

78. Jones, M. B., and Pierce, J. M. Time-use auditing: An approach to validating social indicators. Social Indicators Research, 1977, 4(3), 289-315.

After distinguishing three basic meanings that "perceived life quality" may have, the authors define "quality of life" as objective social conditions necessary to the general happiness, where "happiness" is understood in the broad sense, as including all forms of intrinsically valuable experience, not just "feeling happy." The argument is then made that in order for this definition to be fully implemented, happiness in the broad sense must also be assessed. The latter half of the paper is devoted to describing a set of procedures, collectively called "time-use auditing," for determining the extent to which a person is happy (in the broad sense) in a stated interval of time. Intrinsically valuable experience is analyzed into two dimensions: duration and level. The first is determined by time-budgeting and the second (in a general way) by Maslow's hierarchy of needs. Specifically, Maslow's hierarchy is spelled out in concrete terms by means of "time-use rating structures," each one specific to a particular time-use category. By way of illustration, an audit of three weeks in the life of a 16-year-old girl is presented. The paper concludes with a discussion of what remains to be done, with special stress on writing time-use rating structures for various age groups and modifying structures already in existence to reflect the values of particular social groups.

79. Mason, W. M., Taeuber, K. E., and Winsborough, H. H. Old data for new research: Report of a workshop on research opportunities and issues in the design and construction of public use samples from the 1940 and 1950 censuses and from current population surveys from 1960 forward, held in Madison, Wisconsin, June 28-30, 1976 (CDE Working Paper 77-3). Madison: University of Wisconsin Center for Demography and Ecology, 1977.

The authors describe the issues discussed and positions taken with respect to these issues at a workshop on the design and use of public use data files derived from major data collection efforts (e.g., U.S. Census). Although many files of this sort have yet to be created, discussants focused on key issues related to the development of time-series (or social indicator) data in the following areas: fertility analysis, education, race and ethnicity, labor force, household and family, migration and population, and income. The importance of the recovery and use of all possible years of the Current

Methodological Approaches (MA)

Population Survey is underscored by a brief discussion of the need for time-series data in the development of macro and micro social indicator models and in replication models. The final chapter in this monograph presents recommendations for the creation of public use files and outlines a workplan for accomplishment of this task.

80. Moon, M., and Smolensky, E. (Eds.). Improving measures of economic well-being. New York: Academic Press, 1977.

This collection of papers considers the problems involved in measuring economic welfare. Of particular concern is the way in which such measures could serve policymakers. The majority of articles attempt to define who the poor are among the population. A related, and to some extent inseparable, issue that is addressed is the ranking of families by economic status and the equality of the resulting distribution. Improvements in measuring these attributes, which are especially relevant to vertical equity considerations, also help to guarantee horizontal equity. While emphasis is on ensuring static horizontal and vertical equity, some of the research centers on revising measures of economic status to maintain the quality of equals across space, demographic characteristics, and time.

81. Murray, C. A. A behavioral study of rural modernization: Social and economic changes in Thai villages. New York: Praeger, 1977.

This volume examines the effects of modernization on the quality of life in Thai villages. Forty-two villages are considered, and two major indices are developed. The personal investment index, an index of modernization, measures the frequency of those behaviors that imply expanding aspirations and a favorable attitude toward change. The civic investment index, a measure of the functional capacity of a village, registers those behaviors that are evidence of voluntary, continuing, and widespread villager activity in support of the public good. Detailed examination of the villages showed that unchanneled exposure to modernization can drastically decrease the functional capacity of a village in the absence of countervailing public policy. The volume concludes with an argument for preserving the decentralized organization represented by the village.

82. Robinson, J. P. How Americans use time: A social-psychological analysis of everyday behavior. New York: Praeger, 1977.

This work defines four modes of analyzing time-use data and then applies two of these modes to the analysis of data from a national sample. A social-psychological framework is developed in which time-use is considered to have four kinds of determining factors: personal, role, resource, and environmental. All of these factors are treated as mutually interactive, and time-use itself is viewed as affecting future time-use. This framework is applied to both obligatory and leisure-time activities. The book concludes by suggesting future directions in time-use research.

83. Shin, D. C. The quality of municipal service: Concept, measure, and results. Social Indicators Research, 1977, 4(2), 207-229.

This article presents a discussion of the concept of quality of municipal services. Based upon the argument that service quality is a subjective and collective experience of the citizenry, the quality of municipal service is conceptualized as the interaction of two components: (1) the level of citizen satisfaction with the service and (2) the extent of variation in the distribution of service satisfaction across neighborhoods within a community. To measure these two components, Indices of Service Adequacy and Service Quality are constructed. The indices are used in the analysis of survey data collected from three middle-size Illinois cities in order to assess and compare their service qualities in the areas of police protection, street maintenance, and public education. The measurement proved to be sensitive to intercity and intracity variations in satisfaction in a reasonable and understandable way, which may justify developing more sophisticated forms of the measure. The findings indicated that in these three cities public satisfaction with schools, streets, and police services was relatively low and varied greatly between neighborhoods (defined on the grounds of racial composition) and between cities.

ANALYZING AND REPORTING
SOCIAL INDICATORS

1. Hyman, H. H. Secondary analysis of sample surveys: Principles, procedures, and potentialities. New York: John Wiley & Sons, 1972.

    This book is a basic text on secondary analysis. Chapters I-II consider the benefits of secondary analysis and display the relations between secondary analysis and primary research. Chapter III describes the work styles of successful secondary analysts and in so doing provides an overview of the field. Chapters IV-V present the basic principles and procedures of secondary analysis in the context of relatively simple problems. Chapters VI-VII discuss these basic principles and procedures in greater detail and case studies are examined. Concluding chapters discuss cross-national studies and provide a directory of statistical archives.

2. Sofranko, A. J., and Bealer, R. C. Unbalanced modernization and domestic instability: A comparative analysis. Beverly Hills, California: Sage Publications, 1972.

    This study aims to integrate two major areas of inquiry in the comparative study of societal development: (1) the nature of modernization and (2) the origin and incidence of societal instability. A society is considered as a system of institutional sectors: the political, the economic, and the educational. Regression techniques are used to calculate the discrepancy between the (actual) level of modernization in a sector and the predicted score for that sector based on the levels of modernization in other sectors. Instability is defined in terms of the incidence of war, riots, work stoppage, and civil disobedience. The principal conclusion is that imbalances both within and among sectors are linked to greater domestic instability.

3. Szalai, A. The use of time: Daily activities of urban and suburban populations in twelve countries. The Hague: Mouton, 1972.

    This volume is a report of the Multinational Comparative Time-Budget Research Project. Part I describes the organization, methodology, and theoretical approach of the project. Part II is a collection of articles presenting various aspects of the data collected. Part III presents selected data tables reflecting variations in the duration, frequency, timing, and sequencing of the daily activities of urbanized populations and of subgroups of those populations in twelve countries. Part IV is a bibliography of international publications bearing on time-budget research.

4. United States Department of Health, Education, and Welfare, National Center for Health Statistics. Statistics for comprehensive health planning. Washington, D.C.: The Public Health Conference on Records and Statistics, 1972.

    This document presents a tentative set of guidelines for the use of statistics in comprehensive health planning. The document discusses (1) the role of statistics in health planning, (2) the integration of data, (3) health statistics, (4) demographic and socioeconomic statistics, (5) health manpower statistics, (6) health facilities data; (7) health service statistics, and (8) the organization of statistical activities for environmental health planning.

5. Anderson, J. G. Causal models and social indicators: Toward the development of social systems models. American Sociological Review, 1973, 38, 285-301.

This paper reports on an effort to derive a set of social indicators for the health care area. A structural equation model is constructed for the health care system serving the state of New Mexico. The model specifies relationships hypothesized as existing among social, demographic, and economic variables related to the availability and use of health services and to health status. A set of structural equations indicates the direct effect of variables in the model on each endogenous variable, and a set of reduced form equations indicates the combined direct and indirect effect of each predetermined variable on each endogenous variable included in the model. The author suggests that the model can be used to monitor and explain the effects of changes in particular variables on all other variables composing the health care system. Moreover, he suggests that predictions of the effects of alternative health care policies affecting the provision, organization, or use of health care services can be made on the basis of the model.

6. Cooper, H., Michaelson, J., Shoemaker, P., and Young, G. Social indicators and urban decision-making. Austin, Texas: Lyndon B. Johnson School of Public Affairs, 1973. (NTIS No. SHR-0000224)

A community analysis research project is described that was carried out in 1973 to assess the applicability of social indicators to urban decisionmaking. The approach adopted for the project addressed the following research priorities: (1) assessment of the state-of-the-art regarding social indicators; (2) determination of social statistics available to local governments and local government sophistication in employing this information for decisionmaking purposes; (3) critique of consultant products marketed in the region that are aimed at describing community conditions; and (4) identification of social indicators that describe urban quality of life in a broad sense rather than those that reflect the performance of a limited number of governmental programs. Both research methods and findings for each of these research priorities are discussed. An introductory set of community indicators applicable to cities in the southwest region is provided. Individual community indicators are explained, along with a delineation of the selection rationale used in choosing them. Particular urban decisionmaking applications for the indicators are outlined, and the cost of introducing the indicators to a city of moderate size is estimated. The viability of an indicator approach is examined, as is the analytical potential of community indicators. Strategies are proposed for introducing community indicators to urban decisionmakers. (NTIS)

7. Follettie, J. F. Within and beyond the formative and the summative: An evaluation perspective for large-scale educational R&D. Los Alamitos, Calif.: Southwest Regional Laboratory for Educational Research and Development, 1973. (ERIC No. ED 126 016)

   This paper schematizes large-scale educational research and development (R&D) as a progression of operations and presents a perspective for evaluating those operations and their outputs. Most perspectives thus far presented for evaluation of educational R&D are oriented to small-scale operations and modest products. Prevailing views of formative and summative evaluation, as developed by Scriven, are analyzed in terms of the state-of-the-art for use of social indicators in isolating first-order and higher-order program effects. Implications of the perspective for educational policy, R&D, and the full-service school are presented. Major dimensions of an evaluation perspective are examined along with organizational and individual roles in improving productivity. Some of the chapters characterize the complex educational product and cause-effect progressions pertinent to complex evaluations. It is concluded that independent evaluation is required for all evaluations conducted for a sponsor. The best interest of a development organization will be served by independent evaluators working under contract. There will not be any other kind of evaluation of higher-order effects until a system of social indicators is developed, evaluated, and appropriately institutionalized. (ERIC)

8. Keller, E. Politicizing statistics. Dissent, 1973, 20(2), 142-145.

   This editorial stresses the importance of disseminating social statistics that accurately reflect current trends. It suggests that the government underplays momentarily unfavorable statistics, and it questions the misleading language in which many statistics are reported. Examples that are provided include (1) the discontinuance of reporting unemployment statistics separately for low-income areas in central cities (since December 1971), (2) substituting the term "low-income" for "poverty," and (3) the cancellation, in 1971, of monthly press briefings on the unemployment rate and the Consumer Price Index. The author points out that, though this information is available, it is not made sufficiently accessible to the public.

9. Klages, H. Assessment of an attempt at a system of social indicators. Policy Sciences, 1973, 4(3), 249-261.

   This article evaluates individual chapters in the book Indicators of Social Change (Sheldon & Moore, 1968) in order to assess the extent to which the book contributed to the building of systems of social indicators. The criteria that are used in the evaluation are relevant to the development of such systems and are not concerned with the task of determining which indicators should or should not have been presented. Results of the assessment show that the book scores very low on most of the criteria. While the author praises some of the authors for high scores on several of the criteria, he is critical of the editors of the volume for restricting the size of the publication. In particular, he criticizes their overreliance on descriptive indicators and their disregard for the construction of a system of social indicators that spans more than a simple content area. The author concludes with the negative statement that "the present book provides neither a perspective for further scientific development, nor an aid in making decisions for political-administrative practice, nor a medium of orientation for the public."

10. Parke, R., and Sheldon, E. B. Social statistics for public policy. Proceedings of the American Statistical Association, Social Statistics Section, 1973, 105-112.

The authors argue that it is a mistake to identify the usefulness of social statistics for policy with the question of whether statistics meet the perceived information needs of federal policymakers. Such an identification assumes too great an ability by policymakers to identify their data needs, undervalues the contribution of statistics to the definition and anticipation of problems as distinguished from their solution, and undervalues the role that other constituencies for statistics play in the policymaking process. Alternative criteria for the selection and development of social indicators are suggested.

11. Smith, D. M. The geography of social well-being in the United States. San Francisco: McGraw-Hill, 1973.

The author has carefully examined a wide variety of possible social indicators at different geographic scales and presents the pros and cons of several alternatives. He particularly stresses the need for geographic disaggregation. He argues that, in order to provide effective evaluation of welfare or antipoverty programs, comparable measures must be available not only for an adequate time period, but also at a geographic scale appropriate to the conditions being treated, whether for an inner-city block, a group of low-income rural counties, or a large area such as the Upper Midwest. Many examples are included of the utility of displaying indicators on maps.

12. Bielby, W. T., and Kluegel, J. R. Non-random exogenous variables in path analysis: A comment. American Sociological Review, 1974, 39, 888-891.

The properties of standardized coefficients has been a neglected area in the social indicators literature. The authors' position is that it is incorrect to assert that the consistency of standardized regression coefficients is predicated on the randomness of the exogenous variables. When the exogenous variables are nonrandom, standardized path coefficients are biased for estimating population parameters, but that population parameter for which a standardized path coefficient is consistent is a perfectly respectable parameter to be estimating. The authors conclude that researchers should continue the usual practice of standardizing on the total variance.

Analyzing and Reporting (AR)

13. Blumstein, A. Seriousness weights in an index of crime. American Sociological Review, 1974, 39, 854-864.

    The national index of crime published annually by the FBI is one of the most commonly used social indicators. Many authors have criticized the FBI's index, an unweighted sum of the reported "index crimes," for failing to account for the differing seriousness of the heterogeneous crimes in the index. T. Sellin and M. E. Wolfgang (1962) provided a procedure for developing crime-seriousness weights. An intense public debate has raged over which of these is "correct." This paper compares the FBI and the Sellin-Wolfgang indexes for reported crimes in the United States over the 1962-1972 period; they are found to be almost perfectly linearly related (r=.9994). Thus, the Sellin-Wolfgang index, even though conceptually correct and of value for other purposes, contributes no significant information to a national crime index. Other crime indexes are explored, and most are found to be useful, especially when the mix of crimes remains stable.

14. Bowers, D. G., Franklin, J. L., Drexler, J. A., Jr., and Wissler, A. L. Proceedings of Symposium on the Utilization of Organizational Indicator Data, held on September 25-27, 1974. Ann Arbor, Michigan: University of Michigan Institute for Social Research, 1974. (NTIS No. AD/A-002 273/1ST)

    The report presents the proceedings of the Symposium on the Utilization of Organizational Indicator Data, held in Ann Arbor, Michigan, September 25-27, 1974. Each of the first four sessions covered, in the form of invited papers, a segment of the overall topic: history and background, methodological issues, management information system uses, and developmental uses. The fifth session consisted of a derivation activity, in which general points emerging from the presentations were posted and possible action implications were identified. (NTIS)

15. Christenson, J. A., and Dillman, D. A. An exploratory analysis of select predictors of concern for law and order. Social Indicators Research, 1974, 1(2), 217-228.

    This paper attempts to assess the ability of different variables to predict and explain high concern for law and order. Two aspects of concern are discussed: (1) awareness of crime and (2) willingness to do something about crime. Theoretically, little is known about how awareness for a social problem can be translated into forms of action to deal with the perceived problem. Methodologically, a technique is needed for assessing the relative importance of different variables related to the problem area. Path analysis is discussed as the preferable technique. The data were collected through a random sample of heads-of-households in the state of Washington during the summer of 1970 (N=3,101; response rate = 75%). Some of the major findings include (1) people in larger cities are more aware of a crime problem than people in smaller cities and towns, but people in larger cities are less willing to allocate tax dollars to combat crime; (2) the size of city, and implicitly the crime rate, is the most important variable for understanding the public awareness of crime; (3) the elderly and those of conservative orientation are more willing to allocate funds to combat crime than the young and liberal, although there exists no difference in their awareness of the problem; and (4) relative exposure to mass media, socioeconomic status, or identification with one's community make little contribution to the understanding of either awareness of crime or willingness to allocate tax dollars to combat crime.

16. Ferriss, A. L. Monitoring and interpreting turning points in educational indicators. Social Indicators Research, 1974, 1, 73-84.

The author claims that most turning points in educational indicators are not cyclical but respond to major societal events. Three examples are presented. (1) The probability of a 10th grader continuing to the 11th grade has increased linearly for 60 years, being affected positively by unemployment and negatively by increase in GNP per capita and by military expansion. (2) Baccalaureate degrees per high school graduate four years earlier declined with the expansion of secondary education following the 1890s, rose after World War I, and fell as the Depression approached. A major turning point occurred after World War II, and the indicator peaked in 1950. (3) A current downward turning point in the school enrollment rate of 18- to 19-year-old males may have been prompted by a change in Selective Service policies granting exemptions to college enrollees. The author argues that interpreting turning points by identifying the forces that underlie and direct them would increase our knowledge of the cause-and-effect sequences that affect the educational system. He suggests that continuously monitoring educational indicators would facilitate the development of policy and programs to adjust to dysfunctional educational trends.

17. Galnoor, I. Social indicators for social planning: The case of Israel. Social Indicators Research, 1974, 1, 27-57.

The author views social planning as an organizing framework for guiding government intervention in social life and social indicators as providing the informational basis for formulating policies, preparing social plans and evaluating the impact of government activities. Social planning and social indicators are only two links in a desired sequence of organized social action, but given the urgency of social problems and the opportunity cost of waiting for further theoretical development, the author urges that initial efforts be directed at developing social indicators for social planning. Israel's experience is presented as an example of (1) the ideological and operational background of specific types of intervention by the state and (2) specific areas that have been neglected, or that have not been given adequate attention, because of the lack of social indicators to assist in acquiring an overall understanding of societal changes. These examples are used as a basis for suggesting some practical possibilities of developing social indicators and social planning in Israel and elsewhere. The author lists several implications of his study of the Israeli situation. (1) Social indicators cannot be value-free. (2) National societies, especially in new nations, emphasize the importance of creating and preserving the national framework, often at the cost of internal social development. (3) Narrowly defined economic objectives cannot be assumed to be a "stage" of social development. (4) Sectoral planning in the areas of agriculture, transportation, education, and in other areas related to societal well-being tends also to use an economic and physical information basis. (5) The threshold leading to the industrial and postindustrial era poses some difficult choices for many countries. (6) The detection of societal changes cannot be achieved without a system of social mapping, based on the collection and utilization of social indicators. (7) Policymaking in many countries utilizes various kinds of information on foreign relations, security, economic development, and public opinion. (8) Social reports by an independent organization or by the central government can help in crystallizing this information for purposes of reviewing social changes, pointing out desired directions of social development, and evaluating policy achievements. (9) Government departments and public organizations can use social information for planning and evaluating the social benefits of their activities. (10) The multiplicity of sources of social indicators within any society should be regarded as a safety valve against the totalitarian implications of collecting and using social indicators for social planning. (11) Social indicators and social reports do not guarantee improved social policy and planning.

18. Jones, E. T. The impact of federal aid on the quality of life: The case of infant health. Social Indicators Research, 1974, 1(2), 209-216.

Federal grants-in-aid have been a major device for stimulating new programs for improving the quality of life in the United States. This paper assesses the impact of one such grant-in-aid (Maternal and Child Health Services) on improvements in infant health in the 1950-1964 period. The analysis indicates that the amount of increase or decrease in a state's Maternal and Child Health Services grant had no systematic overall impact on later changes in that state's fetal, neonatal, and infant mortality indicators. In addition, such grant changes had no major systematic impact when controlling for per capita income, changes in per capita income, population, innovation tendencies, and administrative professionalism. The author concludes that the findings provide further evidence that "placing money in one end of the pipeline is no guarantee that the desired results will flow out of the other end." This finding highlights the difficulty a national government has in attempting to change important aspects of the human condition by the use of grants-in-aid.

19. Koshal, R. K., and Koshal, M. Air pollution and the respiratory disease mortality in the United States: A quantitative study. Social Indicators Research, 1974, 1, 263-278.

The authors develop a model relating the respiratory mortality rate to levels of various forms of air pollution, population density, average percentage of days with sunshine, and average humidity. When fitted to time-series data using regression analyses, the model accounts for half of the variance in respiratory mortality rates between cities. The model parameters imply that a doubling of air pollution would increase the respiratory disease mortality rate by 51%-58% and a halving of air pollution would decrease the mortality rate by 25%-29%. In terms of reduction of both mortality and morbidity rates for respiratory diseases alone, the latter would imply a social savings of $1.9-$2.2 billion per year. The annual social savings would be even larger when considering in addition the reduction in other, nonrespiratory, diseases related to air pollution.

20. Kunzel, R. The connection between the family cycle and divorce rates: An analysis based on European data. Journal of Marriage and the Family, 1974, 36, 379-388.

This paper tests the hypothesis that the socioeconomic structure of a country influences the family phases and through these has an effect on divorce rates. All European countries (28 countries) were classified into two groups according to their level of industrial development, and data appropriate for characterizing the phases of the family cycle were compared between the two groups of countries. The findings are that the changes in the family cycle associated with industrialization (falling age of marriage, rise in life expectancy, decreasing number of children, and the growing absorption of women by the labor market) correlate with a rise in divorce rates.

21. Michalos, A. C. Strategies for reducing information overload in social reports. Social Indicators Research, 1974, 1, 107-131.

The author discusses information overload as it relates to the reporting of social indicators and presents 17 suggestions of what to do or not do to reduce information overload. Suggestions include distinguishing between positive, negative, and unclear indicators and eliminating some or all of the unclear indicators; constructing positive and negative indicator indexes (e.g., the percentage of indicators that changed in a favorable direction); converting descriptive data to monetary-value statements, when possible; clearly separating input and output indicators in a report; deleting all but one of any set of highly correlated time series; developing probability-of-dysfunction statements and probability-of-shortage statements and aggregating them to form risk-of-disaster indexes and risk-of-shortage indexes; and developing global indicators to replace aggregations. The author disagrees with some prior suggestions for ways of reducing information overload.

22. Van Dusen, R. A. (Ed.). Social indicators 1973: A review symposium. Washington, D.C.: Social Science Research Council Center for Coordination of Research on Social Indicators, 1974. (ERIC No. ED 108 987)

Following the publication of Social Indicators 1973, a review symposium met to discuss and evaluate the potential utility of the document. The articles in this book present the essence of the commentary at the symposium. Section 1 identifies the themes in the symposium discussions and provides an overview of the proceedings. Sections 2 and 3 place the publication in the context of other publications of national reports on basic social conditions. Comparisons are made between the social trends publications of Sweden, Norway, France, England, West Germany, and the United States. Section 4 reviews the statistical and methodological problems and procedures in such a large data collection of social indicators. A list of symposium participants and a comprehensive list of references cited in the four articles concludes the book. (ERIC)

23. Barabba, V. P. Avoiding future shock: The role of social indicators and social observation. NUEA Spectator, 1975, 39(22), 25-28.

A system of social reporting, developing from the interchange of national and local data, is seen as possible by the National Census Bureau, and development of such a system is discussed. National, regional, and local decisionmakers would benefit from the quick dissemination of data from social indicators systems. (ERIC)

24. Basilevsky, A. Social class and delinquency in London boroughs. Social Indicators Research, 1975, 2, 287-313.

Early empirical studies carried out in the United States of geographically distributed or "ecological" delinquency rates have tended to stress the importance of environmental, attitudinal (anomic) variables, and institutional factors as the principal determinants of urban delinquency. More recent research, however, has indicated that delinquency is highly related with socioeconomic status, rather than with purely ecological factors or with anomie. In the present paper, the authors present new evidence, based on published data, on the causal structure of delinquency in metropolitan London boroughs by means of a combined use of regression analysis and factor analysis. It is found that 50% of the variance of London annual delinquency rates is explained by two indicators of socio-economic status used as independent regression variables. In addition, when social class is controlled for, half of the remaining variance is accounted for by indicators of urban land use and postwar population mobility. Thus, 75% of the total observed delinquency variance is explained by the regression equation. Housing conditions and the extent of nonwhite immigration were found to have no independent effect on delinquency. The author does note, however, that it was difficult to infer a causal structure of delinquency on the basis of the intercorrelated explanatory variables, since the effects of individual variables could not be separated. Finally, the quantified indicators provide a useful typology of London boroughs that permits a characterization of urban areas in terms of their crimogenic properties.

25. Caplan, N., Morrison, A., and Stambaugh, R. J. The use of social science knowledge in policy decisions at the national level: A report to respondents. Ann Arbor, Michigan: University of Michigan Institute for Social Research, 1975. (NTIS No. PB-244 759/7ST)

A study on the use of social science knowledge in the formation of government policy was conducted among 204 upper-level persons in the executive branch of the United States government. Respondents were chosen from agencies representing the entire range of governmental activities. Section I of this report is concerned with findings on the diversity, characteristics, and extent of the knowledge used and with the kinds of impact produced. Section II analyzes the factors that influence the level of knowledge use. Section III presents social indicators of well-being. (NTIS)

26. Center for Social Research and Development, Denver University. Research utilization and the Social Indicators Project. Denver: Author, 1975. (NTIS No. SHR-0000103)

An overview of the development and the activities of the research utilization of the Social Indicators Project is presented in this report. The development of research utilization evolved from a minor byproduct of the project to a major focus of staff concern. It occurred naturally from users' increased awareness of project publications and interest in relating project outcomes and insights to their own specific problems. Working through workshops, seminars, and meetings, the staff developed a linkage role, serving as disseminators and translators of specialized information to potential users, fostering their understanding of the data and increasing the likelihood of effective utilization. Plans for FY 1974-1975 include scrutinizing data used in workshops and meetings to judge effectiveness and possible necessary alterations, performing special limited data analyses, developing projections or trends, providing computer mapping on a limited basis, and other expanded activities. (NTIS)

27. D'Agostino, R. B. Social indicators: A statistician's overview. Social Indicators Research, 1975, 1, 459-484.

In this article, the problem areas of social indicator research that are of concern to the statistician are considered. Among these are the purposes of social indicators, what social variables should be considered as conceivable variables related to quality of life, what data should be collected (taking into account the difficulty of not being able to directly measure variables of interest), how one collects the data (which is usually in the form of a time series) guarding against multicollinearity, and how the collected data should be handled and analyzed. The author discusses why in social indicator research the secular trends, cyclical movements, seasonal variations, and irregular fluctuations must be taken into account. Techniques are discussed for relating lead indicators in one time period to coincident indicators in another period. Finally, a select bibliography is presented on canonical correlation, forecasting, indicators and index numbers, path analysis, regression analysis, simulation techniques, time series analysis, and other areas useful in analyzing social indicator data.

28. Duncan, O. D. Does money buy satisfaction? Social Indicators Research, 1975, 2, 267-274.

There was no change in the distribution of satisfaction with the standard of living among Detroit area wives between 1955 and 1971, although current-dollar median family income more than doubled and constant-dollar income increased by forty percent. Cross-sectional variation in satisfaction is, however, related to income and, in particular, to relative position in the income distribution. Whereas regressions of satisfaction on income in current or constant dollars, or the logarithm thereof, suggest that at the same income there was less satisfaction in 1971 than in 1955, there is no significant year effect in the equation using the income-position variable. Easterlin's thesis that rising levels of income do not produce rises in the average subjective estimate of welfare is supported. The relevant source of satisfaction with one's standard of living is having more income than someone else; not just having more income. To the extent that this is true, satisfaction measures cannot tell us whether a population with a higher average income is really "better off" than a population with a lower one. The author suggests that the same principle might be found to apply to other domains of perceived life quality besides the material level of living and that it may be necessary to develop an "expectations index" for purposes of statistical deflation of subjective purpose.

29. Educational Testing Service. Educational indicators: Monitoring the state of education. Princeton, New Jersey: Author, 1975.

This volume is a collection of six papers that were presented at an invitational conference on educational indicators. The papers include (1) E. B. Sheldon, "The Social Indicators Movement," (2) D. D. Gooler, "The Development and Use of Educational Indicators," (3) S. B. Withey, "Quality of Life as an Educational Outcome," (4) M. Olson, "Measurement and Efficiency in Education," (5) W. J. Cohen, "Educational Indicators and Social Policy," and (6) S. J. Mushkin and B. B. Billings, "Measures of Educational Outcomes in Developing Countries."

30. Elliott, E. Social indicators and program evaluation. Paper presented at the Adult Education Research Conference, St. Louis, Missouri, 1975 (ERIC No. ED 110 852)

The paper examines social indicators as a way of evaluating macro-level adult education programs. in general, social indicators deal with social factors that affect the quality of life of the population-on. Social scientists are recognizing the need for both economic and social indicators. Even as the need for social indicators is discussed, the problems that may be associated with their use (questions of measurement, the reduction of social indicators into economic terms, the definition of quality of life) are recognized. Typical social indicators include health, public safety, education, employment, income, housing, leisure and recreation, and population. In assessing adult education programs with respect to social indicators, the time factor seems to be crucial. In a model evaluation, the procedure moves from focusing on a social concern (one source of program objectives) to identifying appropriate social indicators, to collecting evidence, to referring back to the social concern, and the cycle starts again, presumably at a more advanced point in relation to the social concern. All adult educators need to work to establish evaluative procedures that attend to qualitative as well as quantitative aspects of program output. (ERIC)

31. Ferriss, A. L. National approaches to developing social indicators. Social Indicators Research, 1975, 2, 81-92.

The social indicators reported in ten national publications released to date are primarily measures reflecting public policy and social concerns. The orientation of the volumes from the United States, France, Canada, Norway, the Philippines, Malaysia, and Great Britain are discussed. The selection of time series that reflect social processes is proposed, and an orientation presented around the concepts of the vital processes (birth, death, etc.), socialization and participation, mobility and stratification, maintaining security, and control and coordination by which social order is attained. A bibliography identifies the national reports known to the author.

32. Fienberg, S. E. Perspective Canada as a social report. Social Indicators Research, 1975, 2, 153-174.

This paper reviews the first attempt at social reporting in Canada, Perspective Canada, contrasting it with social reports from other nations, in particular the United States publication, Social Indicators, 1973. A list of 12 changes and improvements for Perspective Canada is suggested, and the paper concludes with a discussion of the importance of the bold use of model building in the analysis of social indicators data and the innovative use of graphical methods for social reporting.

33. Glass, G. V., Willson, V. L., and Gottman, J. M. Design and analysis of time-series experiments. Boulder, Colorado: Colorado Associated University Press, 1975.

This work is an attempt at an integrated treatment of the methodological developments related to time-series experimental design during 1966-1974. Subjects include time-series experiments and the investigation of causal claims, variations on the basic time-series experimental design, estimating and testing intervention effects, sources of invalidity in time-series experiments, concomitant variation in time-series experiments, and spectral analysis of time-series. The book is a technical treatment that builds on the work of G. E. P. Box and J. M. Jenkins (Time-Series Analysis: Forecasting and Control, 1970).

34. Koshal, R. K., and Koshal, M. Crimes and socioeconomic environments. Social Indicators Research, 1975, 2, 223-227.

The article presents a regression model of crime rates as a function of per capita personal income, the unemployment rate, the

Analyzing and Reporting (AR)

migration rate, racial imbalance, average annual temperature, and males as a percentage of the total population. Analyses are presented for total crime rates, property crime rates, and rates of crimes against persons, based on data from 73 standard statistical metropolitan areas in the United States for 1970. Property crime rates are found to be affected by the unemployment rate, climate, per capita personal income, and the migration rate. In contrast, rates of crimes against persons are found to be affected by racial imbalance (negatively), per capita personal income, and the proportion of the population that is male. The authors note that unemployment is an important controllable variable in determining crime rates and that unemployment involves greater social loss than is usually considered.

35. Krishnan, P., and Sangadasa, A. Stochastic indicators of occupational mobility, Canada: 1951-1961. Social Indicators Research, 1975, 1, 485-493.

   This study is concerned with the estimation of Canadian occupational mobility from aggregate census data. The process of occupational mobility is characterized as a stationary Markov chain, and certain meaningful conditions are imposed on the transition probabilities to convert the estimation strategy into a linear programming problem. Cross-section data for 1951 and 1961 are employed for estimation purposes. The study reveals that in 1951-1961, the Canadian females had higher rates of mobility than the males.

36. Land, K. C., and Spilerman, S. (Eds.). Social indicator models. New York: Russell Sage Foundation, 1975.

   In order to explore the notion of a social indicator model in various substantive contexts and relative to several uses, a Conference on Social Indicator Models was held at the Russell Sage Foundation in July 1972. The conference was attended by over 20 social scientists, and, for the most part, the chapters in this volume are the products of those scholars. The chapters are collected into two groups: (1) replication models built on the basis of data from repeated cross-sectional sample surveys and (2) longitudinal and dynamic models based on repeated observations on the same individuals or structural units.

37. Newman, S. Objective and subjective determinants of prospective residential mobility. Social Indicators Research, 1975, 2, 53-63.

   The increasing interest in subjective as well as objective measures of well-being raises the issue of the relative importance of these two different types of measures when they are included as independent variables in analytical or predictive models. In this article, results of a survey are used to evaluate the relative importance of objective and subjective indicators in providing an understanding of why households desire to move. The data upon which the analysis is based were collected in 1971 as part of a national survey of the quality of life in the United States. In contrast to much of the previous research on mobility in which single communities or special subgroups within the population have been studied, these data provide information from a randomly selected, representative sample of more than 3,000 households across the United States. Overall, it is found that subjective indicators add considerably to the explanation of mobility inclinations over and above that contributed by objective indicators. A comparison of explanatory powers for the full sets of objective and subjective predictors within two length-of-residence subgroups indicates some interesting differences, however. Objective and subjective predictors are close in explanatory power for longer-term residents, while subjective measures are considerably more important for shorter-term residents.

38. Scheer, L. A comparison using perceptual indicators: Job satisfaction. Social Indicators Research, 1975, 2, 1-8.

This article presents the results of an Austrian-German comparison pertaining to different aspects of job satisfaction. The German survey took place in six stages between August 1972 and March 1973, and involved a sample of 2,451 full-time employed persons and 3,349 persons who were not employed full-time. The Austrian survey sample included 761 full-time employed persons and 1,239 persons who were not employed full-time. The greatest degree of satisfaction was expressed in both countries for those aspects of the job pertaining to the working atmosphere, including contact with co-workers and superiors. It is argued that, even at this early stage in their development, perceptual indicators can be used to reveal overall trends and to point up trouble spots where socioeconomic action on the part of the authorities is called for.

39. Schneider, M. The quality of life in large American cities: Objective and subjective social indicators. Social Indicators Research, 1975, 1, 495-509.

The concept of "quality of life" as a tool of comparative social indicators research is analyzed. Intercity comparisons of objective and subjective measures of well-being are presented, and the distinctiveness of these two dimensions of the quality of life is documented. In fact, no relationship was found between the level of well-being found in a city as measured by a wide range of commonly used objective social indicators and the quality of life subjectively experienced by individuals in the city. Life satisfaction of individuals appears to be independent of the physical conditions of the cities in which they live. The author suggests that the distinction between objective and subjective indicators should be carefully maintained in future social indicators research.

40. Seidman, D. Simulation of public opinion: A caveat. Public Opinion Quarterly, 1975, 39(3), 331-342.

Recent research on the determinants of policy outcomes in American states and on related matters has employed simulated state-level public opinion data. Simulation methodology is critically examined: its assumptions are evaluated, its computation procedures are shown to be unnecessarily complicated and inaccurate, and its estimates are proved to be logically confounded with the socio-demographic factors that define them. Thus, simulation data cannot be used to investigate the role of public opinion in the policymaking process. (PSYCH ABS)

41. Bilski, R. Basic parameters of the welfare state. Social Indicators Research, 1976, 3, 451-470.

The article attempts to show the limitations and dangers of using the relation between GNP and social security spending as a predominant social indicator for the modern welfare state. The claimed positive correlation between economic growth and percent of social security spending is shown not to be supported by the data. Analysis of the welfare policies of various countries, showing the influence of ideology and strategy on the degree and kind of welfare, calls into question the assumptions of convergence of welfare policies in rich countries and of ideology's lack of influence.

42. Campbell, D. T. Focal local indicators for social program evaluation. Social Indicators Research, 1976, 3, 237-256.

An important role for social indicators is in the evaluation of the impact of specific social programs. This requires (in the absence of randomized experiments) extended time-series of social indicators. Such series will usually only be available for administrative records (both public and private). It is in the national interest that these be made flexibly research-retrievable by local region, by frequent time interval, and in fine topical breakdown. The ability to report aggregate statistics retrieved for lists of persons adds still greater precision in program evaluation and can be done with no loss of privacy and without any release of individual data. For this purpose, the use of uniform individual identification numbers adds efficiency without increased risk to privacy. The author suggests that privacy legislation should be carefully scrutinized to determine whether or not it needlessly precludes such procedures.

43. Caplan, N., and Barton, E. Social Indicators 1973: A study of the relationship between the power of information and utilization by federal executives. Ann Arbor, Michigan: University of Michigan, Institute for Social Research, 1976.

The main purpose of this research report was to assess the use of Social Indicators 1973 (U.S. Office of Management and Budget, 1973) in policy-related decisions among upper-level federal executives. More broadly, the report explores the use of social indicator data in general by comparing the use of SI '73 with background data collected earlier from the respondents. A sample of 202 policymakers was interviewed concerning their needs for social indicator data just before SI '73 was released and again a year later concerning their awareness and use of SI '73; 68 other policymakers were included only in the second series of interviews. The findings are related to process and organizational factors that influenced utilization.

44. Collazo, A. Forecasts of selected social indicators of educational outcomes and recommended policy changes. Tallahassee, Florida: Department of Education, Project on Social Indicators, 1976. (ERIC No. ED 131 583)

This report has three objectives: (1) to identify social indicators relating to policy concerns of the legislature, state board of education, and commissioner of education; (2) to predict the future status of selected social indicators, using the assumption that present policies will be continued; and (3) to recommend policy changes for achieving more desirable futures in selected areas. Section 2 of the report presents the social indicators that were identified and the criteria that were used in their selection. Section 3 presents the forecasting model developed, while Section 4 includes a description of the procedure used in identifying the variables affecting the indicators used in the model. Section 5 contains forecasts of the future status of selected social indicators and a description of the cross-impact analysis methodology used in making the forecasts. Section 6 includes listing of the issues that might have an impact on education and the alternative policy decisions that were proposed to meet changes created by these issues. Section 7 contains recommendations regarding alternative policy decisions along with some recommendations regarding goals of education in Florida and the process of formulating educational policy. (ERIC)

45. Ewusi, K. Disparities in levels of regional development in Ghana. Social Indicators Research, 1976, 3, 75-100.

The objective of this study is to construct a composite index from a number of socieconomic indicators, to bring together relevant data on the socioeconomic variables for all regions of Ghana, and to measure and rank more precisely the regions of the country according to their level of development. The author stipulates criteria for choosing indicators to measure social development, and ten variables related to development are chosen. The Wroclow Taxonomic Method for classifying a set of objects into more or less homogeneous subsets without the use of regression or correlation analysis is described. This technique is used to classify the regions of Ghana into four levels of social development. The main weakness of the taxonomic technique is that each variable is assigned equal weight in the construction of a composite index.

46. Felson, M. E. The differentiation of material life styles: 1925 to 1966. Social Indicators Research, 1976, 3, 397-421.

The relevance of consumer behavior to social differentiation is considered, and its independence from income is documented. Earlier studies of household consumer traits by Sewell and others are taken as baseline data and are compared to the 1966 Detroit Area Study. In the baseline data, published between 1925 and 1940, high correlations were observed among consumer traits. The 1966 study revealed similar relationships among similar traits. Taking correlations and factor loadings as social indicators, material life styles appear to have become more differentiated. After assessing the robustness and relevance of this inference, the author discusses how trends in material life styles may run counter to other social trends. In particular, he suggests that as culture becomes more homogeneous with respect to language and customs, it may become heterogeneous with respect to life styles, especially material life styles.

47. Franco, R. Latin American typology: An essay on measuring social discontinuities. Social Indicators Research, 1976, 3, 275-372.

The purpose of this essay was to develop a detailed classification system for the countries involved in the Latin American Institute of Economic and Social Planning. To accomplish this, the author (1) reviewed and analyzed the extant literature on relevant typological strategies, (2) selected and discussed particular social indicators and methodological procedures, and (3) constructed indicator profiles for the various countries. On the basis of these profiles, measures of the differences among countries were made and a typology was established.

48. Gore, P. H. Quality of life assessment. Torun, Poland: World Congress of Rural Sociology, 1976. (ERIC No. ED 137 026)

Explaining the use of overlay methodology in the assessment of rural social service, this paper describes a technique of visual juxtaposition wherein information is matched with geographic location. To ascertain whether senior citizen centers are located in areas of client concentration, for example, this model superimposes the location of senior citizen centers on the actual distribution of persons aged 65 and over. Presenting an example of the overlay technique as applied to a national study of quality of life involving nine indexes, this paper includes graphic illustrations of the technique. A further example of this technique as applied to a rural development project in Clinton County, New York, is presented to illustrate the way in which four major phases of investigation (census and background data, crossroads survey, key informant survey, and general sample survey) can be compared via the overlay method. On the basis of the work presented in this paper, the following recommendations for assessing rural service needs are made: (1) assemble all pertinent census and secondary data; (2) map the data by geographic location; (3) conduct a survey to identify actual locations of services; (4) interview key informants about where local residents go for services and what particular services are needed; and (5) assemble all the data on overlay maps and present to local decision makers. (ERIC)

49. Harries, K. D. A crime based analysis and classification of 729 American cities. Social Indicators Research, 1976, 2, 467-487.

In this article, thirty social indicators, consisting of crime rates and variables that may be regarded theoretically as correlates of crime, are factor analyzed for 729 incorporated American cities with a minimum population of 25,000. Factors associated with crime, poverty, native-born status, city revenue, residential stability, home construction, city size, and population age are identified. The data matrix is partitioned in order to identify high-crime and low-crime cities. The cities in each category are then subjected to cluster analysis on the basis of the seven socioeconomic factors, and the resulting groups are investigated further in order to identify distinctive clusters and underlying patterns of social conditions. A group of "model" low-crime communities is identified--virtually all were incorporated "white noose" suburbs of metropolitan areas. Residential instability and large population size are associated with two of the high-crime groups, which include stereotypical crime problem cities such as Detroit, Chicago, and Kansas City. The member cities constituting each of the eight groups are listed. The author states that the policy of combating crime primarily through improving the effectiveness of police departments is pursued without particular regard for managerial considerations such as marginal productivity or opportunity costs. The reasons given for this are that dollars allocated to law enforcement provide political catharsis and that no effective measures of law enforcement productivity have been devised. The author is in favor of positive programs, not simply law enforcement, aimed at crime reduction in black communities, but concedes that positive programs are less viable politically than the law enforcement escalation approach currently practiced.

50. Knapp, M. R. Predicting the dimensions of life satisfaction. Canterbury, England: Kent University, Personal Social Services Research Unit, 1976.

A four-equation multiple regression model for predicting life satisfaction in the elderly is developed. Following a discussion of the multidimensional concept of well-being, the sample and instruments used to gather the data on which the model is based are described. Data were gathered from 23 males and 28 females, aged 62 to 86, residing in their own homes in a coastal resort in southern England. The four endogenous variables of the model are four dimensions of life satisfaction: mood tone, zest for life, congruence between desired and achieved goals, and resolution and fortitude. The exogenous variables include several biographical and activity indicators used in earlier gerontological research. The model is estimated by means of a stepwise regression technique in which the exogenous variables are introduced as regressors in the order suggested by their coefficients of correlation. The results indicate that the pattern of regressor influence varies greatly from equation to equation, thereby providing fairly specific evidence on a number of hypotheses concerning predictors of life satisfaction. In particular, the activity perspective on aging appears to be important in predicting mood tone but of little relevance for the other dimensions of life satisfaction. Limited support for the disengagement theory of aging is also provided. Supporting data and a list of references are included. (NTIS)

51. Koshal, R. K., Gallaway, L. E., and Akkihal, R. G. Determinants of male and female higher education in the United States. Social Indicators Research, 1976, 3(1), 111-121.

In this paper, an attempt is made to estimate separately the male and female demand functions for higher education in the United States and to determine which variables affect the degree of demand differentially for the two sexes. Data for 45 of the states were accessed from the Digest of Educational Statistics, 1971, the Comparative Guide to American Colleges, 1972, and the Statistical Abstract of the United States. Ordinary least squares regression was used to estimate separate demand functions for male and female enrollment. In order to determine the relative importance of variables on male and female enrollment, partial enrollment elasticities with respect to these variables at their mean values were calculated. The results suggest that there is no significant difference between the responsiveness of male and female enrollment in terms of the explanatory variables except for the rate of return of higher education. Male enrollment is responsive to such market changes, while female enrollment appears to be independent of this variable. The elasticities with respect to tuition and family income suggest that parents in general do not discriminate between male and female children in terms of sending them to institutions of higher education.

52. Land, K. C., and Felson, M. E. A general framework for building dynamic macro social indicator models: Including an analysis of changes in crime rates and police expenditures. American Journal of Sociology, 1976, 82, 565-604.

In this paper, the authors argue for a revival of analyses of social change based upon time series of indices of social conditions. To provide a general paradigm for this type of analysis, descriptions are given of (1) an opportunity-structures theoretical framework for generating specifications of equations of dynamic macro social indicator models, (2) a demographic accounting framework for grounding such equations in population stocks and flows, and (3) a structural equation strategy for estimating and evaluating the resulting models. To illustrate this paradigm, analyses of three equations determining changes in the national reported property crime rate, the reported violent crime rate, and the rate of public police expenditures are presented. The equations fit annual 1947-72 time-series data well, yield theoretically meaningful coefficients, and lack demonstrable autocorrelation of disturbances. Moreover, the conditional forecasts of the 1973 values of the reported-crime rates fall well within bounds set by the standard errors of the equations.

53. Madduri, V. B. N. S. Stochastic indicators of income mobility. Social Indicators Research, 1976, 3, 423-429.

Income mobility is one of the indicators of social mobility. This study explains the methodology in estimating the stochastic indicators of income mobility in Canada using aggregate time series data. Assuming stationary finite Markov chain approximation of the mobility process, the probabilities of transition from one of five income strata to another were estimated. The absolute minimum deviation criterion was employed for the period 1946-72. The annual average upward income mobility of the Canadian taxpayer was found to be 3.7 percentage points, the downward mobility about one percent, reducing the overall mobility to approximately 2.5 percent. This investigation suggests that, on an annual basis, there was a low degree of upward income mobility in Canada.

54. Martineau, W. H. Social participation and a sense of powerlessness among blacks: A neighborhood analysis. The Sociological Quarterly, 1976, 17(1), 27-41.

   This paper examines the relationship between four types of social participation (formal participation, neighboring, friendship, and extended familism) and a variant of alienation (sense of powerlessness). Data were collected in 1967 from 532 black residents in a depressed neighborhood in South Bend, Indiana. The findings suggest a refinement and reanalysis of the relationships implied by much of the literature, which is usually based on white populations. The strong inverse correlations between participation and alienation found among white populations were not found for this population of blacks. The authors suggest that stability and other characteristics of a neighborhood may be critical variables mediating the relationship and that some of the basic assumptions in this field should be reexamined for black populations.

55. Schneider, M. The "quality of life" and social indicators research. Public Administration Review, 1976, 36, 297-305.

   Objective social indicators, those based on reports or situations that are traits of communities, and subjective social indicators, those based on survey research reports about life experiences and subjective evaluations of life conditions made by individuals, are compared both discursively and statistically in this article. The author points out that too often it is assumed that the more readily available data associated with objective indicators (e.g., from census reports) can be used by themselves to assess life quality; in short, that the physical and psychological aspects of life quality are blurred. The degree of correlation between these two types of indicators is examined empirically using data from analyses of objective conditions in 13 cities made by the Urban Institute, supplemented by U.S. Census data, and reanalyses of the 1968 inter-city survey conducted by Campbell and Schuman for the National Advisory Commission on Civil Disorders. Results suggest that objective social indicators are of little use in understanding quality of life as it is subjectively experienced.

56. Shryock, H. S., Siegal, J. S., and Stockwell, E. G. The methods and materials of demography: Condensed edition. New York: Academic Press, 1976.

   The present work is a condensed and updated version of the two-volume work The Methods and Materials of Demography, first published by the U.S. Bureau of the Census in 1971. Like the original two-volume work, this work attempts to present a systematic and comprehensive exposition, with illustrations, of the methods used by technicians and research workers in dealing with demographic data. The book is concerned with how data on populations are gathered, classified, and treated to produce tabulations and various summarizing measures that reveal the significant aspects of the composition and dynamics of populations. It sets forth the sources, limitations, underlying definitions, and bases of classification, as well as the techniques and methods that have been developed for summarizing and analyzing the data. This book is intended to serve both as a classroom text for courses on demographic methods, aimed at instructing students in how to use population data for analytic studies, and as a reference for professional workers who have occasion to use population data. The sections on population dynamics (natality, reproductivity, marriage and divorce, internal migration, and mortality), population estimates, and population projections are apt to be of particular interest to social indicators researchers.

57. Tropman, J. E. The social meaning of social indicators. Social Indicators Research, 1976, 3, 373-395.

The author argues that, while new modes of data processing have provided reams of data, there has been relatively less effort in seeking to comprehend the social meaning of results of empirical work. A set of previously developed indicators of urban social structure is examined for its link to theory and to the social structure of the city. The original indicators (size, social class, racial composition, and community maturity) were empirically derived. In this paper, each is taken in turn and explored with respect to several possible social meanings. Size, for example, is considered to be an imperfect indicator for system complexity; percent nonwhite is seen to be an indicator for a slowdown in the mobility process or a slower social metabolism. These and other results are suggestions, with illustrations, but do not have conclusive support from other than the original data. While it is hoped that the theoretical suggestions may themselves be of interest, it is also hoped that the approach indicates the fertility and usefulness of going back to theory once empirical measures have been developed.

58. Dever, G. E. A., and LaVoie, M. R. Practical computer graphics for planning health policy. Social Indicators Research, 1977, 4(2), 119-162.

Computer-generated graphics have been successfully employed in various disciplines. However, computer graphics are just beginning to be utilized in the health field. Advantages and disadvantages of computer graphics are listed. Computer graphics are relatively inexpensive to produce once front-end hardware and software are installed. They are accurate, versatile, and can produce production-ready copies in minutes. The authors contend that health information can be better understood by health program managers and decision-makers through the use of computer-generated graphics.

59. Felson, M. E., and Land, K. C. Social, demographic, and economic interrelationships with educational trends in the United States: 1947-74. (Working Paper in Applied Social Statistics No. WP7610) Urbana, Illinois: University of Illinois at Urbana-Champaign, Department of Sociology and Social Science Quantitative Laboratory, 1977.

This paper presents a 34-equation model linking trends in educational enrollments, attainments, and organizations to one another and to certain social, demographic, and economic trends for the United States during the years 1947-1974. The model-building strategy employed integrates many of the ideas of Stone's demographic accounting approach.

60. Foster, R. Economic and quality of life factors in industrial location decisions. Social Indicators Research, 1977, 4(3), 247-265.

In late 1974 and early 1975, a four-page questionnaire was mailed to businessmen in North America. Three samples were drawn: the first included firms in selected industries in the United States, the second surveyed firms in the same industries in Canada, and the third surveyed firms in all industrial classifications in Canada. The three samples surveyed 8,846 industrial firms, one of the largest mail surveys of businessmen undertaken. The questionnaire dealt with economic and quality of life variables that might be considered when deciding whether and where to relocate. In addition, respondents were asked to indicate if their quality of life had gotten better, remained the same, or gotten worse in recent years. Also, respondents from the selected Canadian industries survey were asked to indicate if their current quality of life was satisfactory or unsatisfactory. Businessmen in all three surveys were asked what economic factors they would trade off for an improved quality of life, and, if they were to relocate, what geographic area of the United States or Canada they would choose. The responses showed clearly that a majority of businessmen believed that the quality of life for themselves and their key employees and the daily operation of their plant had improved. In addition, a majority of Canadian respondents from the selected industry survey believed that their quality of life was satisfactory. The surveys also documented the quality of life and economic variables considered important by the respondents.

61. Land, K. C., and Felson, M. E. A dynamic macro social indicator model of changes in marriage, family, and population in the United States: 1947-1974. Social Science Research, 1977, 6(4), 328-362.

The authors present an integrated 21-equation model of how marriage, family, and population conditions, as indexed by macro social indicators, affect each other and are affected by other social, demographic, and economic forces. An opportunity structures theoretical paradigm is applied to the specification of dynamic structural equations for determining changes (both trends and cyclical fluctuations) in marriage formation and dissolution, family and household composition, fertility, mortality, population growth, and population distribution. The equations are estimated on annual national data for the United States during the post-World War II years 1947 to 1972, and then they are used to make conditional forecasts of the values of some of the endogenous variables for 1973 and 1974. It is found that the equations fit the observed data well, lack demonstrable autocorrelation of disturbances, and forecast the 1973 and 1974 values usually with less than 2% error. Strategies are sketched for further refining some of the equations, and it is suggested that this model should be integrated into a larger societal model so that some of the social consequences in other institutional areas from changes in marriage, family, and population can be documented.

62. Land, K. C., and Pampel, F. C. Indicators and models of change in the American occupational system, 1947-73: Some preliminary analyses. Social Indicators Research, 1977, 4, 1-23.

This paper extends earlier conceptual and empirical work by Bell, Lebergott, and Moore on changes in the American occupational system in the post-World War II period. After updating and extending several time series of occupational indicators used by these authors and adding some others as well, the authors specify and estimate a number of dynamic structural-equation models to explain changes in the occupational system as indexed by the social indicators. These equations indicate that (1) Bell's thesis about a shift from a production of goods orientation to a performance of services orientation in postwar American society needs to be qualified; (2) the shift is due to increased productivity in agriculture rather than in industry; (3) increased bureaucratization of employment results, in part, from the shift out of agriculture and other postwar trends in the technological and organizational context of the work environment; and (4) societal investments in military technology and in scientific research and development have had an important impact upon the occupational system in terms of shifting upwards the distribution of occupations with respect to prestige. In each of the topics analyzed, the authors make suggestions for developing additional indicators and for refining the structural equations. In addition, the potential of these equations for social forecasting is considered.

63. Pampel, F. C., Land, K. C., and Felson, M. E. A social indicator model of changes in the occupational structure of the United States: 1947-74. American Sociological Review, 1977, 42(6), 951-964.

This paper presents a 10-equation dynamic structural equation model that shows how changes in the occupational structure of the United States affect each other and are affected by economic, technological, and institutional conditions. The model postulates a recursive flow of causation (no explicit feedback relationships) from changes in sectorial (agricultural, manufacturing, services) demand and productivity to changes in the distribution of occupation by sector, bureaucratization, and status level. Application of the model to data from past years (1947 to 1972) allows conditional forecasts to be made and validated against new data. The equations fit the observed data well, lack demonstrable autocorrelation of disturbances, and forecast the 1973 and 1974 values with considerable accuracy. While changes in sectorial demand and productive efficiency were substantial during the 1947-1972 period, the rates of change in these driving variables of the model have decreased in the 1970s. If these rates of change continue to decline, then the model leads to the prediction that there will be a contraction in the rate of growth of high status jobs, which in turn implies a decline in the rate of upward occupational mobility in the absence of other counterbalancing structural changes.

64. Ratner, R. S. A modest Magna Charta: The rise and growth of Wage and Hour Standards laws, 1900-1973: A social indicators approach. Washington, D.C.: Employment and Training Administration, Office of Research and Development, 1977. (NTIS No. PB-273 926/6ST)

The report investigates growth of Wage and Hour Standards legislation in the United States. A social indicators approach was used to measure change in the provisions of these laws. The author reviews statues for a 28-state sample and for the federal government between 1900-1973 and generates a set of time-series data. The author analyzes both the national pattern of change in these laws and the pattern of change at the state level. The author then investigates the correlates of legislative change: (1) determinants of variations in coverage under these laws; (2) correlates of congressional voting on the Fair Labor Standards Act; and (3) the relationship between economic changes, unionization, and growth of social reform. Finally, theoretical and historical positions concerning social reform in 20th-century America are assessed. (NTIS)

65. Rodgers, W. L. Work status and the quality of life. Social Indicators Research, 1977, 4(3), 267-287.

The general thesis from which this paper is derived is that objective conditions are related to perceptions and evaluations of those conditions, but that such relationships are mediated by personal characteristics such as expectation and aspiration levels and other motivational factors. The specific relationship examined is that between work status and overall life satisfaction among women. Although there is little difference in average levels of life satisfaction expressed by housewives and by women working outside the home, substantial differences emerge when women are distinguished by their motivation with respect to paid work: among women who want jobs, working women are more satisfied with their lives than are housewives; while among those who would prefer not to work, housewives are more satisfied. Evidence is also found in support of a hypothesis that work tends to be less central to the overall quality of women's lives than is true for men. Working women are less likely than working men to be committed to the work role, and a higher proportion of women than of men say that they would not work at all if they did not need the money. Most of the dissatisfaction of unemployed women, unlike unemployed men, can be explained in terms of their below-average family incomes.

66. Taeuber, C. (Ed.) America in the 70s: Some social indicators. Annals of the American Academy of Political and Social Science, 1978, 435.

This issue of the Annals was prepared under the special editorship of Conrad Taeuber. It is a collection of interpretive essays based on individual chapters of Social Indicators 1976. Among the individuals who contributed articles are Robert Parke, David Seidman, Arthur Campbell, Murray Weitzman, Abbott Ferriss, Barbara Carter,

John Robinson, and Denis Johnston. In addition to presenting conclusions based on examination of the data included in Social Indicators 1976, the authors offered comments and criticisms regarding the volume. While Social Indicators 1976 was regarded, generally, as an informative compilation of statistical data, concerns were noted for the lack of data in selected areas, the absence of cautionary remarks concerning data quality, and the lack of attention to prominent social issues in organizing the data for dissemination. A brief comparison between Social Indicators 1976 and Perspective Canada II was made, and the author concluded that neither volume was entirely successful in developing social indicators or in providing a social report. He concluded that such efforts must, in the future, involve authors from outside the government if they are to have greater success.

67. Zill, N. National survey of children: Summary of preliminary results. New York: Foundation for Child Development, 1977.

This paper presents the results of a preliminary analysis of the data collected by the National Survey of Children. The data are based on interviews of 2,258 children, ages 7 to 11, and of 1,748 of their parents. The results presented describe children's attitudes toward and experience in their homes, neighborhoods, and schools. Some of the specific topics addressed are (1) children's attitudes toward violence, (2) styles of reward and punishment in childrearing, (3) neighborhood improvements suggested by children, (4) attitudes toward tests at school, (5) attitudes toward being male or female, (6) attitudes toward being black, (7) mothers' attitudes toward childbearing, (8) the incidence of unplanned children, and (9) the general physical and mental health of the children surveyed. The results in this last topic area are compared with those of the 1963-1965 National Health Examination Survey. Where significant, correlations are reported between the various attitudinal measures and factors such as socioeconomic status of parents, race, sex, degree of parental education, and rural vs. suburban vs. urban residence. The summary concludes with a brief description of the survey sample.

EXAMPLES OF SOCIAL INDICATORS
USED OR IN USE

1. Bass, B. M., and Franke, R. H. Societal influences on student perceptions of how to succeed in organizations: A cross-national analysis. Journal of Applied Psychology, 1972, 56, 312-318.

    The authors administered the Organizational Success Questionnaire to a total of 1,009 college students in the United States, Britain, the Netherlands, France, West Germany, and Sweden. Results support the hypothesis that national social indicators would help account for differences in endorsement of social (participative) and political (manipulative) intervention for organizational success. Compared across nations, students' opinions of behavior requisite for business success tended to be similar to attitudes of managers, but opposed to childhood values. Endorsement of social approaches appeared related nationally to social flexibility and per capita wealth, while endorsement of political approaches appeared related negatively to these but positively to social division and inequality of income distribution. Support of frequent intervention (social or political) was related to national social division and to rapid growth of per capita wealth. An integrative model is suggested. (PSYCH ABS)

2. Bureau of Labor Statistics. Selected papers from the North American Conference on Labor Statistics. Washington, D.C.: Author, 1972. (ERIC No. ED 076 804)

    This document comprises 15 research-based speeches presented at the North American Conference on Labor Statistics by students and leading authorities in the field. Among the prevailing themes were (1) labor statistics and their relationship to life styles; (2) women laborers, sex discrimination, and provisions for working mothers; (3) recent research conducted on social indicators and their relationship to the labor market; (4) blacks in the building trades; (5) inflation--its effects and implications to labor; (6) wages and productivity in the United States and Canada; and (7) the status of the labor market as it relates to the teenager as a potential member of the labor force. (ERIC)

3. Executive Office of the President: Office of Management and Budget. Social indicators 1973: Selected statistics on social conditions and trends in the United States. Washington, D.C.: U.S. Government Printing Office, 1973.

    The book contains statistics selected and organized to describe social conditions and trends in the United States. Most of the data were compiled through federal government surveys. The following eight major social areas are examined: health, public safety, education, employment, income, housing, leisure and recreation, and population. Within each of these categories, areas of social concern are identified. The concerns selected reveal the general status of the entire population, depict conditions that are, or are likely to be, dealt with by national policies, and encompass many of the important issues facing the nation. Indicators show the status of the population in relation to each particular concern. The indicators presented are restricted almost entirely to data about objective conditions and are primarily time series showing national totals. In almost every case, the national totals are disaggregated to show the age, sex, and racial characteristics of the population. Each of the eight chapters contains a brief text, charts, technical notes, and tables. Sources for data shown in the charts are given in the tables. (ERIC)

4. Moore, W. E., and Crowe, M. J. Urban social indicators: Selected conditions and trends in Denver and its metropolitan area. Denver: Denver Urban Observatory, 1973. (NTIS No. PB-223 919/2)

The report explores the kinds of data available that could be utilized for the development of social indicators of urban change in Denver and the Standard Metropolitan Statistical Area and serves as a part of an intercity program to develop urban social indicators on a comparative basis, which will permit comparisons among a group of cities in the Urban Observatory network. The areas of social concern for which indicator information is presented are physical environment (air pollution), health, public safety, education, housing, and employment and income, with special emphasis given to employment indicators. (NTIS)

5. Morrissett, I. Some kind words for the GNP. Social Education, 1973, 37, 605-609.

The relationship between quality of life and the GNP is the focus of this article, which defends the GNP. Four positive propositions about economic growth and the GNP are stated and defended. It is acknowledged that there is a need for social indicators broader than the GNP accounts. (ERIC)

6. Mushkin, S. J., and Stageberg, S. National Assessment and social indicators, January 1973. Washington, D.C.: Georgetown University Public Services Lab, 1973. (ERIC No. ED 082 290)

National Assessment of Educational Progress is a survey of how much United States citizens know about and what they are capable of doing in ten broad subject areas. This pamphlet outlines the types of findings on educational achievement that might be made from the statistical data on knowledge, attitudes, and skills being gathered. Additionally, the report examines social indicators that could be developed from the data, explores the use of National Assessment data for the understanding of educational achievement, and considers how National Assessment might contribute to a measurement of the quality of life. (ERIC)

7. Organization for Economic Cooperation and Development. A framework for educational indicators to guide government decisions. Paris: Author, 1973. (ERIC No. ED 106 212)

Mainly dealing with proposals concerning indicators for measuring the impact of education on society, this report attempts to present a framework of educational statistics related to the main policy concerns of member countries. Indicators are assessments of the condition of society vis-a-vis its aspirations and goals. The report defines some of the more important general policy objectives and examines statistical measures that are most useful to monitor progress or regression within each area of concern. This approach admits that indicators of performance must be multidimensional so that education can meet its many objectives, including contributions to the transmission of knowledge, equality of opportunity and social mobility, meeting the needs of the economy, individual development, and transmission and evolution of values. Finally, the effective use of resources in pursuit of the policy objectives is discussed. (ERIC)

8. Palys, T. S. Social indicators of quality of life in Canada: A practical/theoretical report. Winnipeg: Manitoba Department of Urban Affairs, 1973.

The work of Michael J. Flax is used to compare conditions in ten Canadian urban centers. The author's purpose is not to assess quality of life, but rather to test the usefulness of Flax's approach and to propose the type of data gathering and research that must be done in connection with studies of quality of life. Results show that the statistics available were too ambiguous for accurate interpretation, too unreliable, and, in many cases, bordered on complete invalidity. It is concluded that criteria must be developed by which potential indicators can be judged. The author proposes that research be initiated in which representative population samples are interviewed regarding their perceptions of the reality in which they live. Also, more specific focus for indicator studies (e.g., census tract within city versus citywide) is called for, and three methods for collecting indicator data are described.

9. von Otter, C. Sociology in the service of politics: Comments on the Swedish Level of Living survey. Acta Sociologica, 1973, 16, 229-238.

Social indicators research is in itself a social indicator of some interest, and the author suggests that it is relevant to ask what caused current interest in the social indicators movement. He concludes that a demand for social indicators is derived from the need to supplement the market-mechanism and its inability to direct attention and efforts to (1) the problems of groups that are unimportant and marginal from an economic point of view, (2) those aspects of life where prices do not adequately express needs or preferences, (3) secondary effects of market directed development, and (4) certain long-range effects. The author reviews the 1968 Level of Living Survey in Sweden and criticizes the selection of indicators. He concludes that the indicators should have been based on social theory, but commends several aspects of the survey.

10. Watts, W., and Free, L. A. State of the nation. New York: Universe Books, 1973.

This book is the report of a survey that used a "self-anchoring striving scale" and was conducted by Potomac Associates. The survey was performed during FY 1971-1972. The aim of the survey was to determine the public opinion of Americans with respect to current national events. Procedures of the survey are presented along with measures of public attitudes toward major events.

11. Edwards, B. Sources of social indicators. London: Heinemann, 1974.

This book is a guide to and review of statistical material available from official sources in England on topics of social concern. The annotated references of source documents are divided into five content areas: (1) population and vital statistics, (2) health, welfare, and social security, (3) housing, (4) education, and (5) crime and justice.

12. Hastings, P. K. (Ed.). Survey data for trend analysis. Washington, D.C.: Social Science Research Council, Center for Coordination of Research on Social Indicators, 1974.

This book is an index to all questions asked in two or more years in the American national survey holdings of the Roper Public Opinion Research Center. Each entry consists of the question wording, the survey organization that asked the question, the number and date of the survey, and the number of the question. The same information is provided for variant wordings of the question. The index provides sufficient information to permit quick identification of survey data items likely to be useful in constructing time series. As an aid to researchers undertaking secondary analysis of survey data, a short guide to survey archive research is included.

13. Goldsmith, H. F. Demographic norms for metropolitan, nonmetropolitan, and rural counties: Mental health demographic profile system working paper no. 24. Rockville, Maryland: National Institute of Mental Health, 1975. (ERIC No. ED 141 010)

Utilizing 1970 census statistics for metropolitan, nonmetropolitan, and rural counties, this paper presents the selected percentile values for the 130 statistics (social indicators) in the Mental Health Demographic Profile System. The MHDPS is a system that allows the delineation of residential areas with common social rank, life style, ethnicity, and other related characteristics and permits inferences regarding social service needs among comparable populations. The MHDPS contains indicators of the major components of the social rank dimension--economic status, social status (occupation), and information status (education); the life style dimension--family status, family life-cycle stage, residential life style, and familism; and ethnicity dimensions--community stability, area homogeneity, and populations with high risk of social problems. (ERIC)

14. Hauser, P. M. Social statistics in use. New York: Russell Sage Foundation, 1975.

The purpose of this book is to provide the educated lay reader with information on how statistics, especially those collected and compiled by government, are used, and in so doing to show justification for the census, government surveys, and other statistical undertakings that require public cooperation. The focus is mainly on social, as distinguished from economic, statistics, although the boundary line is not always clear and the statistics examined often have both social and economic implications. A number of experts were asked to prepare memoranda on the nature and uses of data in their fields of specialization, and the memoranda were then edited and rewritten into a nontechnical and uniform style by the author. The book is divided into chapters on thirteen content areas as well as chapters on the need for statistics, on public opinion polls, and on social indicators.

15. Hill, R. B. The implications of poverty statistics for minorities. The New York Statistician, 1975, 27(1), 9-10.

This article offers detailed criticism of the official poverty standard that was current in 1975 on the grounds that it was insensitive to the consumption patterns distinctive of low-income racial minorities (e.g., the disproportionate expenses that low-income groups incur for rent). It was pointed out that because of the insensitivity of the measure, many families were being excluded from services that they vitally needed.

16. Hobson, R., and Mann, S. H. A social indicator based on time allocation. Social Indicators Research, 1975, 1, 439-457.

This article presents a social indicator, called Lambda, that has as its base the manner in which individuals allocate their time among various life activities. Lambda is a weighted sum social indicator with both subjective and objective aspects. The weights are decided by the population under consideration and not by the investigators or some other outside agents (hence the authors argue that Lambda does not suffer from experimenter bias). The elements to be summed are the frequencies of discrepancies between the amount of time individuals state they would like to spend in an activity versus the amount of time they say they actually spend in the activity. The properties of this indicator are discussed in detail. A pilot study comparing Lambda to another social indicator (reported happiness--a measure used by Gallup in 1949 and 1971) and some demographic variables was conducted with 1,012 undergraduate students. Findings from the study were that (1) males and females rated themselves equally on reported happiness, but females rated considerably lower than males on Lambda (i.e., there were more discrepancies reported by women between desired and actual time use) and (2) Lambda for blacks in the sample was considerably lower than Lambda for whites, but not nearly as low as blacks scored relative to whites on the happiness measure. Lambda is currently being used by the Gallup organization.

Examples of Indicators in Use (EX)

17. Hopkins, C. Program impact estimation for Community Information and Service Centers. (Report No. OTR-75-68) Washington, D.C.: Office of Telecommunications, 1975. (NTIS No. COM-75-11290/4ST)

    The impact of government programs may be estimated (1) by measuring the attitudes of citizens before and after program activation and (2) by noting the change in selected social indicators before and after program activation. This paper describes the application of these procedures to local areas within city governments with emphasis on the installation of Community Information Service Centers (CISCs) using advanced telecommunications technology. A literature survey is included. (NTIS)

18. Johnston, D. F. National social indicator reports: Some comparisons and prospects. Washington, D.C.: General Assembly of the World Future Society, 1975. (ERIC No. ED 109 014)

    This report provides comparisons among the social indicator reports of seven countries: Canada, France, Great Britain, Japan, Norway, the United States, and West Germany. The purpose of social indicator research in each country is to provide a means for developing more adequate answers to questions concerning present and emerging social trends. Limitations of the social indicator reports are that the data are purely descriptive of broadly aggregated trends and can provide only a general perspective of the emerging trends. The appendix is a comparison chart of social-concern coverage reports of the seven countries in areas of social concern including population characteristics; family characteristics; housing and community characteristics; social welfare and security of the population; health and nutrition; public safety and legal justice; education and training; work; income, wealth, and expenditures; leisure, recreation, and cultural activity; social mobility and social participation; and miscellaneous areas. (ERIC)

19. Madden, J. P. Children in Pennsylvania: Volume I, State summary. Social Indicators for Human Services Series, No. 1. University Park: Pennsylvania State University Department of Agricultural Economics and Rural Sociology, 1975. (ERIC No. ED 107 421)

    The first in a series of 53 publications designed to provide information relative to human service decisionmakers, this datebook constitutes a statistical summary of the socioeconomic problems of children and families with children in Pennsylvania's 67 counties. Data taken from the 1970 U.S. Census Report are presented via 24 tables, 15 figures, and 17 maps. Data analyzed by county are presented for the following social indicators: (1) percent of children in poverty; (2) lowest median family income; (3) income deficit per poor family; (4) poor families not receiving wages or salaries; (5) poor families with children and female head, percent of all families; (6) children not living with both parents, percent; (7) infant deaths per 1,000 live births; (8) children in housing lacking complete plumbing, percent; (9) children in overcrowded housing, percent; (10) children 5-6 years old not in school, percent; (11) children 16-17 years old not in school, percent; and (12) males age 16-21, percent not in school and not high school graduates and not employed. Other pertinent data relative to general demographic characteristics (age, ethnic group, and sex), family, health, housing, education, employment, and family income are presented as both number of cases and percents. (ERIC)

20. Martin, G. The French experience of social planning: Evaluation and prospects. International Social Science Journal, 1975, 27, 87120.

Social planning activities in France are described in this article. These activities, referred to as the Sixth and Seventh Plans (1970-1975 and 1975-1980, respectively), involved the definition and use of indicators descriptive of social conditions, social interventions, and the effects of these interventions. Activities of the Sixth Plan are described, and the types of indicators selected for use are presented. The author attributes the failure of the Sixth Plan to an orientation that viewed social groups (e.g., the young, the immigrant population) as isolated units. Thus, the study of the dynamic relations among the groups and between them and society was precluded. Also, at the level of government policymaking, no link was established between the condition of these groups, the objectives pursued in their report, and the means required for attainment of those objectives. These limitations (and the consequent failure of the Sixth Plan) led to attempts to widen the field covered and to systematize the links among indicators in order to arrive at a new form of planning. Thus, the Seventh Plan was developed and a function-oriented planning approach was taken. "Collective functions," which describe activities undertaken with the declared wishes of the nation in one or more of its fields of action (e.g., education, health), are being developed using types of concepts introduced by Sharkansky (1969). The stages in development of these functions are (1) determination of goals in the field of action; (2) identification and measurement of advantages provided by the collective activities and their distribution among types of beneficiaries; and (3) characterization of these activities as output indicators. The author concludes that "the framework of collective functions undoubtedly represents an advance in the sphere of collective decisionmaking." Proposals that are presently being considered by the Seventh Plan are (1) more detailed study and development of social indicators linked to collective functions; (2) establishment of a social report; and (3) broader use of macroeconomic models that, up to the present, have dealt only with limited problem areas. Two appendixes are presented; the first contains a list of social indicators proposed for the field of education, and the second contains an outline of the social report proposed in the Seventh Plan.

21. Ontell, R. The quality of life in eight American cities: Selected indicators of urban conditions and trends. Washington, D.C.: National League of Cities, 1975. (NTIS No. PB245 255/5ST)

The report summarizes the results of a comparative research study of social indicators carried out in eight participating Urban Observatories. It provides a historical overview and theoretical discussion of the principal issues involved in social indicators research, reporting, and monitoring, as well as a discussion of the development and application of specific measures of social conditions in the six

Examples of Indicators in Use (EX)

domains--income and employment, health, education, public safety, housing, and air pollution--selected for investigation. (NTIS)

22. UNESCO. The social indicators programme at UNESCO. International Social Science Journal, 1975, 27, 195-197.

This paper describes the principal work efforts in the social indicators area of the Division of Social Science Methods and Analysis of UNESCO since its first meeting in 1967. Three projects have received the most attention during the past decade: (1) the development of human resources indicators; (2) the identification and use of key indicators of social and economic change; and (3) the development of indicators of the quality of life and of the environment. Major publications based on these efforts are cited, and a list of 35 individual studies carried out within the framework of these projects is presented. Most of the study reports that are cited are obtainable in mimeographed form from UNESCO.

23. United Nations Statistical Office. Toward a system of social and demographic statistics. New York: United Nations, 1975. (United Nations Document ST/ESA/STAT/SER.F/18)

This publication is a technical report on the design of a system of social and demographic statistics. The publication has three parts. The first deals with structural characteristics of the system--its objectives, scope, organization, and procedures. The second part considers the sequences and subparts of the system--their purposes and definitions, basic series and classifications, and social indicators. The third part consists of examples of analyses that have been performed to date.

24. Campbell, A. Subjective measures of well-being. American Psychologist, 1976, 31(2), 117-124.

Traditionally, the "happiness" of the American population has been measured in economic or objective terms. But research indicates that between 1957 and 1972, while the economic and social indicators were rapidly moving upward, the proportion of the population who described themselves as "very happy" declined steadily, particularly among the most affluent portion of the population. It is argued that, in order to describe the quality of the experience of the population, more subjective measures are needed to examine the experience itself. Three general measures of life experience (satisfaction with life, affective quality of life, and perceived stress) are discussed in terms of an earlier study conducted by the author. Findings from that study indicate that, while the three measures are moderately related to each other, people living in different circumstances express different patterns of well-being and these patterns reflect the peculiar quality of the situation in which they live. (PSYCH ABS)

25. Lash, T. W., and Sigal, H. State of the child: New York City.
New York: Foundation for Child Development, 1976.

This report is an attempt to gather and disseminate as much
information as possible about the conditions of New York City
children. Lists of major concerns for children were compiled, compared to the relevant research literature, and reviewed by experts.
In each content area, a search was made for statistical indicators that
were reliable, valid, and of known normative significance and had
been repeatedly measured over some time period. The statistical
tables in the report are usually organized from multiple sources.
Chapters cover the subjects of the characteristics and distribution of
the population of children in the city, their family situations, health,
education, children who do not live at home, foster care, children as
offenders and victims, and the juvenile justice system. In cooperation with the study, community organizations trained teams of lay and
professional members in observation and interviewing techniques and
monitored child-health stations, the public school attendance program,
food programs in the public schools, and bilingual programs in the
schools over six- to nine-month periods. The results of this monitoring are reported in four chapters, followed by a budget analysis that
reviews the public sector investments in essential children's services.

26. Oster, S. A review of the definition and measurement of poverty:
Volume I, Summary review paper; Volume II, Annotated bibliography;
Volume III, The measure of poverty. Washington, D.C.: Department
of Health, Education, and Welfare, Office of the Assistant Secretary
for Planning and Evaluation, 1976. (ERIC No. ED 141 424)

This study reviews the existing literature on a series of issues
associated with the definition and measurement of poverty. It
consists of a summary report covering this research (Volume I) and
an annotated bibliography (Volume II). Eleven specific issues were
identified and reviewed in this study: (1) the historical definitions of
poverty, (2) the use of index numbers in the measurement of poverty,
(3) family size and composition adjustments on measures of poverty,
(4) geographical variation in public service provision by type of
service, (5) regional income differences, (6) wealth and assets and
consumption as measures of poverty, (7) poverty standards and the
consumption of leisure, (8) determinants of the turnover rates of poor
families, (9) social and economic proxies for poverty, (10) social
indicators of poverty, and (11) state administrative definitions of
poverty. The literature in the annotated bibliography was primarily
drawn from the disciplines of economics, sociology, and political
science. Unpublished working papers and doctoral dissertations from
several major universities were also reviewed, as well as a number of
relevant government documents. The literature review showed that
poverty definitions currently used by states in administering their
poverty programs are inadequate, since very little research has been
done in this area. (ERIC)

Examples of Indicators in Use (EX)

27. Van Dusen, R. A., and Sheldon, E. B. The changing status of American women: A life cycle perspective. American Psychologist, 1976, 31(2), 106-116.

A profound change in the status of American women is evident in recent trends in women's educational attainment, labor force participation, and patterns of marriage, divorce, and childbearing. The present article reviews federal statistics that describe these trends, as well as some of the recent social science literature on the status of American women. It is suggested that one way of summarizing these trends is in terms of the declining importance of the family life cycle in a woman's total life cycle, or alternatively, the diminishing social importance of the distinction between married women and those who are unmarried (i.e., never married, no longer married, or not yet married). (PSYCH ABS)

28. Congressional Budget Office. Poverty status of families under alternative definitions of income. Washington, D.C.: U.S. Government Printing Office, 1977.

This analysis was requested by former Senator Walter Mondale of the Senate Budget Committee to aid the 95th Congress in considering legislation to reform social welfare programs. This report provides the basis for evaluating any proposed social welfare program through an analysis of how the current income transfer programs lift families out of poverty. The size of the poverty population is estimated under alternative income definitions, and the effectiveness of cash and in-kind transfer programs in moving families out of poverty is displayed as a function of family type, race and age of family head, and region of the country.

29. Executive Office of the President: United States Department of Commerce, Office of Federal Statistical Policy and Standards, Bureau of the Census. Social indicators 1976: Selected data on social conditions and trends in the United States. Washington, D.C.: U.S. Government Printing Office, 1977.

This volume is the sequel to Social Indicators 1973. It is a comprehensive collection of statistical data, presented in graphic form and descriptive of current social conditions in the United States. The volume contains two new chapters not found in the earlier edition--one on the family, another on social mobility and participation. Overall, the report focuses primarily on indicators of well-being and public perceptions. The graphs are followed by corresponding tables. Citations are given to the data sources from which the indicators are developed. Interpretative essays for each chapter of this volume can be found in C. Taeuber (Ed.), "America in the 70s: Some social indicators," Annals of the American Academy of Political and Social Science, 1978, 435.

30. Mangahas, M. The Philippine social indicators project. Social Indicators Research, 1977, 4(1), 67-96.

The Social Indicators Project of the Development Academy of the Philippines (1974) aimed to formulate a measurement system capable of

113

objectively depicting periodic changes in national development. It identified the following as basic Philippine social concerns: (1) health and nutrition, (2) learning, (3) income and consumption, (4) employment, (5) nonhuman productive resources, (6) housing, utilities, and the environment, (7) public safety and justice, (8) political values, and (9) social mobility. This list is unusual in considering political welfare. A multidisciplinary research team selected 30 major indicators pertinent to these concerns. Among other criteria, they required that the indicators have a strictly monotonic relationship to welfare on a priori grounds and that the indicators measure final, or output, states. (Not all of the indicators meet these criteria.) Although the majority are already encompassed by the Philippine statistical system, certain new indicators were proposed, including disability due to illness, human capital created by schooling, net beneficial product, families below a food threshold, an index of housing adequacy, an air pollution index for Greater Manila, an index of perceived public safety, indices of political mobility and efficacy, and indices of occupational mobility and perceived social mobility. A survey of 1,000 households was used to demonstrate the feasibility of gathering needed new primary data, particularly those attitudinal in nature. An analysis of time series showed that certain aspects of Philippine welfare have been notably improving, but that others have been worsening; the direction of national progress can only be ascertained by using value-judgments of the relative importance of the several components of welfare.

31. Statistics Canada. Perspective Canada II: A compendium of social statistics, 1977. Ottawa: Minister of Supply and Services, 1977.

This volume updates and augments Perspective Canada, published in 1975. For the most part, statistics that are reported were those available in or before 1974, although some indicators of housing, school enrollments, and public media are based on 1975 and 1976 data. Many tables, charts, and maps are presented, and each section addressing an area of concern begins with descriptions of trends in the area, the data that are presented, and definitions of terms that are used to present these data. In addition to addressing standard areas of social well-being (e.g., education, health, housing), statistics are presented to describe the status of the aged, major urban centers, bilingualism, and native peoples.

32. Thayer, N. B. A new social portrait of the Japanese. Wilson Quarterly, 1977, 1(4), 61-72.

A series of surveys performed between 1953 and 1973 assessed postwar attitudes of the Japanese toward religion, tradition, culture, politics, and aesthetics. Findings indicate that Japanese attitudes have become more oriented toward the individual than toward society. (ERIC)

Examples of Indicators in Use (EX)

33. National Center for Education Statistics. The condition of education, 1978. Washington, D.C.: U.S. Government Printing Office, 1977.

 This volume is the 1978 edition of the NCES report on the condition of education in the United States. The volume is principally a compendium of statistical data on students, education personnel, schooling outcomes, school finance, and a comparison between education in the United States and in other countries. The Condition of Education has been published annually since 1975.

BIBLIOGRAPHIES OF SOCIAL INDICATORS RESEARCH

1. Agency for International Development. Social indicators. Washington, D.C.: Department of State, Agency for International Development, 1972.

    This bibliography, designed for use by A.I.D. technicians, contains 92 references to the professional literature on social indicators. Forty-four of the citations are annotated, some extensively so.

2. Wilcox, L. D., Brooks, R. M., Beal, G. M., and Klonglan, G. E. Social indicators and societal monitoring: An annotated bibliography. San Francisco: Jossey-Bass, 1972.

    This bibliography is a selective collection of over 600 annotations from more than 1,000 cited sources. These listings not only give examples in modeling, utilization, and planning, but also assess the movement of social change and suggest means of development. This bibliography has a cross-indexing system, by which author and keyword subject can be located in their taxonomic areas and subject categories. Many of the references have been obtained from the United States, others from European nations, some international organizations, and the United Nations. An address index is included for further communication of ideas. (ERIC)

3. Merwin, D. J. Quality of life: A bibliography of objective and perceptual social indicators. Seattle: Battelle Human Affairs Research Centers, 1976.

    This bibliography is organized into four sections: books, reports and documents, papers, and journal articles. The 146 citations were published during the years 1966 to 1975. (NTIS)

4. PROJECT SHARE (DHEW) and Florida State Department of Health and Rehabilitative Services, Tallahassee. Needs assessment. Rockville, Maryland: Author, 1976. (NTIS No. SHR-0200201).

    A two-part bibliography on needs assessment is presented. The first section contains 200-word abstracts for 25 documents from the PROJECT SHARE collection. Some of the documents deal solely with methodologies for performing needs assessments, while others describe and evaluate results of needs assessment studies. An overview of needs assessment research and methodologies is among the documents abstracted, as are training materials. Accompanying each abstract is a notice of the availability of the document and, where appropriate, of an executive summary from PROJECT SHARE. An alphabetic list of authors is provided. The second section is an annotated bibliography of needs assessment developed by the Florida Department of Health and Rehabilitative Services. Literature in the areas of needs assessment, social indicators, resource assessment, evaluative research, service utilization analysis, and organizational analysis is cited. The

Bibliographies (BB)

listing includes articles describing various methodologies that have been used to assess needs, including the key informant approach, the community forum approach, analysis of existing client records, social indicators analysis, and field surveys of communities or clients. Articles on social indicators describe specific indicators and some of the policy implications of these statistics. Methodological work in the area of resource assessment is represented in other listings, as are evaluation research methodologies and approaches to service utilization analysis. Some of the articles in the section on organizational analysis address significant organizational variables that affect the extent to which needs assessment information will be used. (NTIS)

5. Adams, G. H. Citizen participation in local government: Volume 1, 1964-1973 (a bibliography with abstracts). Springfield, Virginia: National Technical Information Service, 1977. (NTIS No. PS-77/0377/0ST)

    Participation and participative planning in urban administration and municipal affairs by citizens form the basis for this two-volume bibliography. Volume 1 begins the coverage of advisory groups, feedback, involvement programs, leadership efforts, information systems, attitude surveys, social indicators, policymaking, and community structures. Such participation is used in planning and developing projects for housing, health, education, labor, poverty reduction, and economic development. The use of mass media and communication is reported. The bibliography contains 129 abstracts. (NTIS)

6. Adams, G. H. Citizen participation in local government: Volume 2, 1974-April 1977 (a bibliography with abstracts). Springfield, Virginia: National Technical Information Service, 1977. (NTIS No. PS-77/0378/8ST)

    Volume 2 of a two-volume bibliography on participation and participative planning in urban administration and municipal management by the citizenry continues the citations begun in Volume 1. Administration of health care, water resources, human services, coastal zones, community affairs, recreational facilities, criminal justice and crime prevention programs, economic advancement, roads and traffic control, communications, regional transportation, and public policies are among the topics of discussion. The bibliography contains 114 abstracts. (NTIS)

7. Office of Planning and Research, State of California. Putting social indicators to work: An annotated bibliography. Sacramento, California: Author, State of California, 1977.

    This annotated bibliography offers selected sources documenting the application of social indicators at the state and local level. It contains 134 citations.

117

8. Young, M. E. Social indicators (a bibliography with abstracts). Springfield, Virginia: National Technical Information Service, 1977. (NTIS No. 391 812)

The factors that influence life styles and indicate social needs, responses, or conditions for populations are studied. These factors include economic status, health, education, and social organization and are used for governmental planning at all levels. This bibliography contains 61 abstracts. (NTIS)

AUTHOR INDEX

Abrams, M. (MA) 1
Abt, C. C. (MA) 31
Adams, G. H. (BB) 5, 6
Aday, L. A. (MA) 51
Agency for International
  Development (BB) 1
Akkihal, R. G. (AR) 51
Akpom, C. A. (MA) 61
Allardt, E. (TA) 1, 11; (MA) 52
American Philosophical Society
  (TA) 40
Anderson, J. G. (AR) 5
Anderson, R. (MA) 51
Andrews, F. M. (MA) 16, 17,
  53, 54
Anonymous (SA) 17
Arnold, W. R. (TA) 12

Bagley, M. D. (TA) 50
Barabba, V. P. (AR) 23
Barker, R. G. (TA) 13
Barrows, R. L. (MA) 32
Barton, E. (AR) 43
Basilevsky, A. (AR) 24
Bass, B. M. (EX) 1
Baster, N. (MA) 2
Bauer, R. A. (KH) 3
Baumheier, E. C. (TA) 41
Beal, G. M. (BB) 2
Bealer, R. C. (AR) 2
Beardsley, P. L. (MA) 18
Bell, D. (KH) 12 .
Bennett, K. F. (MA) 33
Bharadwaj, L. (MA) 70
Biderman, A. D. (KH) 4;
  (TA) 23; (MA) 55
Bielby, W. T. (AR) 12
Bilski, R. (AR) 41
Blackburn, R. T. (MA) 33
Blakely, E. J. (TA) 68
Blau, T. H. (MA) 71
Blumstein, A. (AR) 13
Bowers, D. G. (AR) 14
Box, G. E. P. (KH) 19
Bradburn, N. M. (TA) 24
Brand, J. (TA) 42
Brenner, B. (MA) 34
Brim, O. G., Jr. (TA) 43
Brooks, R. M. (BB) 2
Brossman, M. W. (SA) 1
Bubeck, A. E. (SA) 2

Bunge, M. (TA) 44, 56
Bureau of Labor Statistics (EX) 2
Bush, J. W. (MA) 3, 20
Buttel, F. H. (MA) 72

Campbell, A. (TA) 2; (MA) 56;
  (EX) 24
Campbell, D. T. (KH) 6; (AR) 42
Caplan, N. (AR) 25, 43
Carmichael, N. (SA) 16; (MA) 19
Center for Social Research and
  Development (AR) 26
Central Statistical Office (KH) 20
Chen, M. K. (MA) 57
Chen, M. M. (MA) 3, 20
Chester, R. (TA) 57
Christenson, J. A. (AR) 15
Christian, D. E. (TA) 25
Citrin, J. (MA) 73
Clark, T. N. (MA) 11, 58
Clemhout, S. (TA) 26
Cohen, W. J. (KH) 10
Collazo, A. (AR) 44
Colley, D. G. (MA) 35
Commission on Critical Choices for
  Americans (TA) 58
Congressional Budget Office
  (EX) 28
Conner, L. I. (TA) 41
Converse, P. E. (TA) 2; (MA)
  47, 56
Cook, C. L. (TA) 41
Cooper, H. (AR) 6
Crandall, R. (MA) 53
Crowe, M. J. (EX) 4

D'Agostino, R. B. (AR) 27
Deichsel, A. (MA) 36
de Neufville, J. (MA) 37
Dever, G. E. A. (TA) 59;
  (MA) 74; (AR) 58
DeWeese, L. C. (MA) 59
Dignan, G. (MA) 38
Dillman, D. A. (AR) 15
Doyle, J. G. (MA) 39
Drewnowski, J. (MA) 4
Drexler, J. A., Jr. (AR) 14
Drury, T. F. (TA) 23; (MA) 55
Dubin, R. (TA) 27
Duet, C. P. (TA) 65
Dumenil, G. (TA) 60

Duncan, O. D. (KH) 13;
 (SA) 10; (AR) 28
Dunn, E. S. (SA) 8

Economic Planning Centre
 (TA) 14
Education Policy Research Center
 (KH) 14
Educational Testing Service
 (AR) 29
Edwards, B. (EX) 11
Edwards, J. (TA) 45
Elinson, J. (TA) 28
Elliott, E. (AR) 30
Environmental Protection Agency
 (TA) 3
Espenshade, T. J. (MA) 21
Evers, S. (MA) 75
Ewusi, K. (AR) 45
Executive Office of the President
 (EX) 3, 29

Fagnani, F. (TA) 60
Fanshel, S. (MA) 3
Fein, R. (SA) 5
Felson, M. E. (AR) 46, 52, 59,
 61, 63
Ferriss, A. L. (KH) 15, 21, 25;
 (AR) 16, 31
Fienberg, S. E. (AR) 32
Finsterbusch, K. (TA) 15
Firestone, J. M. (MA) 5
Fishburn, P. C. (TA) 61
Fishman, J. E. (MA) 12
Fitzsimmons, S. J. (TA) 62, 69
Flanagan, J. C. (TA) 46
Florida State Department of
 Health and Rehabilitation
 Services (BB) 4
Follettie, J. F. (AR) 7
Fontane, P. E. (TA) 47; (MA) 22
Forrester, J. W. (KH) 26
Foster, R. (AR) 60
Fox, K. A. (TA) 29
Franco, R. (AR) 47
Franke, R. H. (EX) 1
Franklin, J. L. (AR) 14
Free, L. A. (EX) 10
Freeman, H. E. (KH) 23; (TA) 4

Gallaway, L. E. (AR) 51
Galnoor, I. (AR) 17
Garn, H. A. (TA) 63

Gilmartin, K. J. (TA) 70
Girardeau, C. (TA) 5, 6
Gitter, A. G. (TA) 16; (MA) 6, 12
Glass, G. V. (AR) 33
Gleser, L. J. (MA) 23
Goeke, J. R. (SA) 11
Goldsmith, H. F. (EX) 13
Gordon, R. A. (MA) 23
Gore, P. H. (AR) 48
Gottman, J. M. (AR) 33
Greenbaum, W. (MA) 76
Gross, B. M. (KH) 5, 16; (SA) 12
Guttman, L. (TA) 49

Hamburger, P. L. (SA) 13
Harries, K. D. (AR) 49
Harvey, A. S. (MA) 60
Harvey, P. (TA) 68
Harwood, P. de L. (TA) 64
Hastings, P. K. (EX) 12
Hauser, P. M. (EX) 14
Henderson, D. W. (TA) 30
Henriot, P. J. (TA) 7
Hill, R. B. (MA) 40; (EX) 15
Hjerppe, R. (TA) 8
Hobson, R. (EX) 16
Hopkins, C. (EX) 17
House, P. (MA) 41
Hubert, J. J. (TA) 71
Hughes, B. (MA) 13
Hughes, J. W. (TA) 9
Hyman, H. H. (AR) 1

Inhaber, H. (MA) 42
InterStudy (TA) 31

Jaeger, R. M. (MA) 77
Jenkins, G. M. (KH) 19
Jenkins, S. (MA) 24
Johnston, D. F. (EX) 18
Johnstone, J. N. (TA) 17
Jones, E. T. (AR) 18
Jones, M. B. (MA) 78
Jung, S. M. (MA) 25

Katz, S. (MA) 61
Keller, E. (AR) 8
Khakhulina, L. A. (MA) 62
King, D. C. (MA) 63
Klages, H. (AR) 9
Kline, K. L. (MA) 68
Klonglan, G. E. (TA) 73; (BB) 2
Kluegel, J. R. (AR) 12

Knapp, M. R. (AR) 50
Knox, P. L. (TA) 32
Kogan, L. S. (MA) 24
Koshal, M. (AR) 19, 34
Koshal, R. K. (AR) 19, 34, 51
Kovenock, D. M. (MA) 18
Krieger, M. H. (TA) 33
Krishnan, P. (AR) 35
Krug, R. E. (MA) 25
Kumagai, T. G. (MA) 9
Kunzel, R. (AR) 20

Land, K. C. (KH) 22, 27;
 (SA) 6, 15; (TA) 48;
 (AR) 36, 52, 59, 61, 62, 63
Lash, T. W. (EX) 25
Laszlo, C. A. (TA) 34
Lavey, W. G. (TA) 62, 69
LaVoie, M. R. (AR) 58
Levine, M. D. (TA) 34
Levy, S. (TA) 49
Lippman, L. (MA) 64
Little, D. (MA) 7
Liu, B. C. (MA) 26, 43
Livingston, R. (MA) 41
Long, C. J. (MA) 63

MacDonald, W. S. (MA) 60
Mack, R. P. (TA) 72
Madden, J. P. (EX) 19
Madduri, V. B. N. S. (AR) 53
Maloney, J. F. (MA) 14
Mangahas, M. (EX) 30
Mann, S. H. (EX) 16
Markley, O. W. (TA) 50
Martin, G. (EX) 20
Martineau, W. H. (AR) 54
Martinson, O. B. (MA) 72
Mason, W. M. (MA) 79
McCall, S. (TA) 51
McIntosh, W. A. (TA) 73; (MA) 75
Merwin, D. J. (BB) 3
Michaelson, J. (AR) 6
Michalos, A. C. (AR) 21
Milbrath, L. W. (MA) 44
Miller, R. B. (SA) 22
Milsum, J. H. (TA) 34
Mondale, W. F. (KH) 7
Moon, M. (MA) 80
Moore, W. E. (KH) 2, 11; (EX) 4
Morrison, A. (AR) 25
Morrissett, I. (EX) 5
Morss, E. R. (TA) 35
Moss, M. (SA) 9

Mostofsky, D. I. (TA) 16; (MA) 6
Murray, C. A. (MA) 81
Mushkin, S. J. (EX) 6

National Center for Education
 Statistics (EX) 33
Newfield, J. W. (TA) 65
Newman, S. (AR) 37
Niitamo, O. E. (TA) 8
Nijkamp, P. (MA) 65

Oborn, P. T. (SA) 3; (TA) 41
Obudho, R. A. (SA) 20
Office of Planning and Research
 (BB) 7
Olkinuora, E. (MA) 15
Olson, M. (KH) 17
Ontell, R. (EX) 21
Organization for Economic
 Cooperation and Development
 (TA) 18, 19; (MA) 66; (EX) 7
Oster, S. (EX) 26

Palys, T. S. (EX) 8
Pampel, F. C. (AR) 62, 63
Parke, R. (SA) 4, 16, 18;
 (MA) 19; (AR) 10
Patrick, D. L. (MA) 20
Peskin, H. M. (MA) 45
Pierce, J. M. (MA) 78
Plessas, D. J. (SA) 5
President's Research Committee
 on Social Trends (KH) 1
PROJECT SHARE (BB) 4

Quinn, R. P. (TA) 36

Rao, M. V. (TA) 52
Ratner, R. S. (AR) 64
Raynauld, A. (TA) 53
Reynolds, W. C. (MA) 18
Riedel, M. (MA) 46
Rivlin, A. M. (KH) 28
Robinson, J. P. (MA) 82
Rodgers, W. L. (MA) 47, 56;
 (AR) 65
Rosenberg, B. (MA) 67
Rossi, R. J. (TA) 70
Rudd, N. M. (MA) 68
Rummel, R. J. (MA) 27
Russ-Eft, D. F. (TA) 46, 70

Sahr, R. C. (MA) 44

Sangadasa, A. (AR) 35
Scheer, L. (AR) 38
Schmid, A. A. (MA) 48
Schneider, M. (AR) 39, 55
Schoggen, P. (TA) 13
Schutz, H. (TA) 68
Schwartz, R. D. (KH) 6
Seashore, S. E. (TA) 37
Sechrest, L. (KH) 6
Seidman, D. (AR) 40
Seminar on Social Indicators (MA) 8
Shaffer, R. E. (MA) 32
Sheldon, E. B. (KH) 2, 11, 23, 29; (SA) 4, 6, 18; (AR) 10; (EX) 27
Shin, D. C. (MA) 83
Shoemaker, P. (AR) 6
Shryock, H. S. (AR) 56
Siegal, J. S. (AR) 56
Siegmann, A. E. (TA) 66
Sigal, H. (EX) 25
Sismondo, S. (TA) 20
Slaughter, E. L. (TA) 41
Smith, D. M. (AR) 11
Smolensky, E. (MA) 80
Sofranko, A. J. (AR) 2
Southern California Association of Governments (MA) 49
Spautz, M. E. (TA) 10
Spilerman, S. (AR) 36
Stageberg, S. (EX) 6
Stambaugh, R. J. (AR) 25
Statistics Canada (EX) 31
Stockwell, E. G. (AR) 56
Stolte-Heiskanen, V. (TA) 38; (MA) 50
Stone, P. J. (MA) 36
Straussman, J. D. (SA) 12
Strumpel, B. (TA) 67; (MA) 28
Sucre, M. G. (TA) 56
Sweney, A. B. (MA) 69
Swinburn, C. (MA) 41
Szalai, A. (AR) 3

Taeuber, K. E. (MA) 79; (AR) 66
Taylor, D. G. (MA) 51
Terleckyj, N. E. (KH) 24; (TA) 54
Thayer, N. B. (EX) 32
Tropman, J. E. (AR) 57
Tubbs, V. A. (MA) 69

UNESCO (EX) 22
United Nations Department of Economic and Social Affairs (TA) 21
United Nations Statistical Office (EX) 23
United States Department of Health, Education, and Welfare (KH) 18; (AR) 4
United States Environmental Protection Agency (TA) 22
United States Senate (KH) 8, 9
Utah Water Resources Laboratory (MA) 29

Van Dusen, R. A. (SA) 14; (AR) 22; (EX) 27
Volgy, T. (MA) 13
von Otter, C. (EX) 9

Wachs, M. (MA) 9
Walton, R. E. (TA) 39
Watts, W. (EX) 10
Webb, E. (KH) 6
Wilcox, L. D. (TA) 55, 73; (MA) 10; (BB) 2
Wilkening, E. A. (MA) 70, 72
Willson, V. L. (AR) 33
Winsborough, H. H. (MA) 79
Wissler, A. L. (AR) 14
Withey, S. B. (MA) 17, 54

Young, G. (AR) 6
Young, M. E. (BB) 8
Young, R. C. (TA) 74

Zapf, W. (SA) 7, 19, 21
Zill, N. (AR) 67
Ziller, R. C. (MA) 30

SUBJECT INDEX

Children (KH) 1; (TA) 40, 43; (MA) 21, 24; (AR) 18, 67; (EX) 19, 25

Crime and justice (KH) 1, 16, 18, 20, 29; (TA) 2, 62; (MA) 23, 46; (AR) 13, 15, 24, 34, 49, 66; (EX) 3, 4, 11, 14, 18, 21, 29, 30, 31

Economy (KH) 1, 11, 26; (SA) 1, 9, 11, 13; (TA) 29, 32, 67; (MA) 32, 43, 60, 65, 80; (EX) 5

Education (KH) 1, 11, 15, 16, 18, 20, 25; (SA) 22; (TA) 14, 17, 18, 52, 62, 65; (MA) 12, 15, 26, 32, 43, 63, 76, 77; (AR) 16, 29, 44, 51, 59, 66; (EX) 3, 4, 6, 7, 11, 13, 14, 18, 21, 27, 29, 30, 31, 33

Employment (KH) 1, 11, 16, 20, 21, 25; (SA) 11; (TA) 2, 14, 23, 24, 27, 36, 37, 39, 48, 52, 62; (MA) 55, 56; (AR) 35, 36, 38, 62, 63, 64, 65, 66; (EX) 2, 3, 4, 13, 14, 18, 21, 27, 29, 30, 31

Family (KH) 1, 11, 21, 25; (TA) 2, 38, 40, 62; (MA) 21, 50, 56; (AR) 20, 46, 61, 66; (EX) 13, 14, 18, 27, 29, 31

Health (KH) 1, 11, 16, 18, 20, 25; (TA) 14, 28, 31, 52, 59, 60, 62, 66; (MA) 3, 6, 20, 24, 26, 31, 32, 43, 51, 57, 63, 74, 75; (AR) 4, 5, 18, 19, 66; (EX) 3, 4, 11, 14, 18, 21, 29, 30, 31

Housing (KH) 20; (SA) 20; (TA) 13, 14, 21, 52, 62; (MA) 26, 44, 56; (AR) 61, 66; (EX) 3, 4, 11, 13, 14, 18, 21, 29, 30, 31

Income and poverty (KH) 1, 11, 16, 18, 20, 21, 25; (TA) 14, 31, 52, 58, 62, 67; (MA) 26, 32, 68; (AR) 28, 36, 53, 66; (EX) 3, 4, 13, 15, 18, 21, 26, 28, 29, 30, 31

Leisure (KH) 1, 11, 20, 25; (TA) 2, 62; (AR) 66; (EX) 3, 14, 18, 29, 31

Physical environment (KH) 1, 16, 18, 20, 26; (SA) 1, 11; (TA) 14, 52, 62; (MA) 29, 42, 43, 44, 45, 65; (AR) 19; (EX) 4, 21, 30, 31

Population (KH) 1, 11, 20, 21, 25, 26; (SA) 11; (TA) 52, 62; (MA) 63, 65; (AR) 36, 56, 61, 66; (EX) 3, 11, 14, 18, 29, 31

Quality of life (KH) 26; (SA) 1, 17; (TA) 3, 16, 22, 32, 44, 46, 49, 51, 58, 64, 65; (MA) 1, 14, 16, 17, 26, 30, 34, 41, 47, 52, 53, 54, 56, 63, 70, 71, 72, 78; (AR) 28, 39, 50, 55, 65; (EX) 8, 24

Religion (KH) 1, 11; (SA) 11; (TA) 58, 62; (MA) 22

Social development (SA) 20; (TA) 9, 11, 15, 55, 68, 69, 74; (MA) 2, 10, 25, 32, 62, 81; (AR) 2, 45

Social mobility (KH) 11, 18; (AR) 36, 53, 66; (EX) 18, 29, 30

Youth (KH) 1, 29; (SA) 11; (MA) 38

**NO LONGER THE PROPERTY
OF THE
UNIVERSITY OF R. I. LIBRARY**